BIG FEELINGS

FEELING EXCITED

by Mary Lindeen

NORWOOD HOUSE PRESS

DEAR CAREGIVER, The *Beginning to Read* Big Feelings books support children's social and emotional learning (SEL). SEL has been proven to promote not only the development of self-awareness, responsibility, and positive relationships but also academic achievement.

Current research reveals that the part of the brain that manages emotion is directly connected to the part of the brain that is used in cognitive tasks such as problem solving, logic, reasoning, and critical thinking—all of which are at the heart of learning.

SEL is also directly linked to what are referred to as 21st Century Skills: collaboration, communication, creativity, and critical thinking. The books included in this SEL series offer an early start to help children build the competencies they need for success in school and life.

In each of these books, young children will learn how to recognize, name, and manage their own feelings while learning that everyone shares the same emotions. This helps them develop social competencies that will benefit them in their relationships with others, which in turn contributes to their success in school. As they read, children will also practice early reading skills by reading sight words and content vocabulary.

The reinforcements in the back of each book will help you determine how well your child understands the concepts in the book, provide different ideas for your child to practice fluency, and suggest books and websites for additional reading.

The most important part of the reading experience with these books—and all others—is for your child to have fun and enjoy reading and learning!

Sincerely,

Mary Lindeen

Mary Lindeen, Author

Norwood House Press
For more information about Norwood House Press please visit our website at www.norwoodhousepress.com or call 866-565-2900.
© 2022 Norwood House Press. Beginning-to-Read™ is a trademark of Norwood House Press.

Editor: Judy Kentor Schmauss   **Designer**: Sara Radka

Photo Credits: Getty Images: LWA, 14, Ariel Skelley, 9, FatCamera, 3, ferrantraite, 21, Images By Tang Ming Tung, 14, 15, Jose Luis Pelaez Inc, 26, Jupiterimages, 10, Khosrork, cover, 1, Maki Nakamura, 15, Marc Romanelli, 14, Michael Prince, 17, MoMo Productions, 29, Robin Bartholick, 18, Robyn Breen Shinn, 5, SanyaSM, 25, SDI Productions, 13, Vladimir Vladimirov, 6, wilpunt, 22

Library of Congress Cataloging-in-Publication Data has been filed and is available at catalog.loc.gov

Library ISBN: 978-1-68450-817-4   Paperback ISBN: 978-1-68404-671-3

What do you do when you feel excited?

Do you clap your hands?

Maybe you smile or laugh when you feel excited.

Or maybe you jump up and down.

Maybe you do all of these things!

There are lots of
ways to show you
feel excited.

There are also lots of reasons to feel excited.

Do you feel excited when you get a good surprise?

Do you feel excited when you get to do something you've been waiting to do?

Do you feel excited when you learn something new?

Different people feel excited about different things.

But everyone feels excited sometimes.

There are times you might
feel just a little bit excited.

Other times you might feel really excited!

And sometimes
you might even feel
too excited.

This can make it hard
to control yourself.

You might talk too
loud or too often.

Your body might feel like it has too much energy.

It can be hard to calm down when you feel too excited.

But there are some things you can do that can help.

Take some deep breaths.

Try talking slower and more softly.

Or shake your hands or move around to get rid of extra energy.

Now you can relax and have fun!

. . . READING REINFORCEMENT. . .

CONNECTING CONCEPTS

CLOSE READING OF NONFICTION TEXT

Close reading helps children comprehend text. It includes reading a text, discussing it with others, and answering questions about it. Use these questions to discuss this book with your child:

1. What does it mean to feel excited?
2. What are some ways to show you feel excited?

Once you have discussed the above questions, ask your child to either draw a picture of someone who is feeling excited or choose one of the children pictured in the book. Then ask the following questions about the child in the drawing or the photo:

1. How can you tell this person might be feeling excited?
2. What might be one reason this person is feeling excited?
3. How would you feel in that situation?
4. Do you ever feel excited? When?
5. When you feel too excited, what do you do? How could someone else help you if you're feeling too excited?

VOCABULARY AND LANGUAGE SKILLS

As you read the book with your child, make sure he or she understands the vocabulary used. Point to key words and talk about what they mean. Encourage children to sound out new words or to read the familiar words around an unfamiliar word for help reading new words.

FLUENCY

Help your child practice fluency by using one or more of the following activities:

1. Reread the book to your child at least two times while he or she uses a finger to track each word as it is read.
2. Read a line of the book, then reread it as your child reads along with you.
3. Ask your child to go back through the book and read the words he or she knows.
4. Have your child practice reading the book several times to improve accuracy, rate, and expression.

FURTHER READING FOR KIDS

Alladin, Erin. *A World of Mindfulness.* Herndon, VA: Pajama Press, 2020.

Anthony, William. *The Yellow Book: What to Do When You're Excited.* Minneapolis, MN: Bearport Publishing Company, 2021.

Holmes, Kristy. *Feeling Excited.* San Diego, CA: Kidhaven Publishing, 2018.

FURTHER READING FOR TEACHERS/CAREGIVERS

Child Development Institute: Coping with Your Child's Personality
https://childdevelopmentinfo.com/child-development/temperament_and_your_child/temp4/#gs.26zje2

Healthline: What Is Sensory Overload?
https://www.healthline.com/health/sensory-overload

Understood: Why some kids get overexcited
https://www.understood.org/en/friends-feelings/managing-feelings/overexcitement/why-some-kids-get-overexcited

Feeling Excited uses the 90 words listed below. *High-frequency* words are those words that are used most often in the English language. They are sometimes referred to as sight words because children need to learn to recognize them automatically when they read. *Content* words are any words specific to a particular topic. Regular practice reading these words will enhance your child's ability to read with greater fluency and comprehension.

HIGH-FREQUENCY WORDS

a	even	new	things
about	get	now	this
all	good	of	time(s)
also	has	often	to
and	have	or	too
are	help	other	up
around	it	people	way(s)
be	just	show	what
been	like	some	when
but	little	something	you
can	make	take	your
different	might	that	
do	more	there	
down	much	these	

CONTENT WORDS

bit	extra	maybe	sometimes
body	feel(s)	move	surprise
breaths	fun	really	talk(ing)
calm	hands	reasons	try
clap	hard	relax	waiting
control	jump	rid	yourself
deep	laugh	shake	you've
energy	learn	slower	
everyone	lots	smile	
excited	loud	softly	

About the Author

Mary Lindeen is a writer, editor, parent, and former elementary school teacher. She has written more than 100 books for children and edited many more. She specializes in early literacy instruction and books for young readers, especially nonfiction.

WICCA
BOOK OF SPELLS

**A BOOK OF SHADOWS FOR
WICCANS, WITCHES & OTHER
PRACTITIONERS OF MAGIC**

LISA CHAMBERLAIN

STERLING ETHOS
New York

STERLING ETHOS
New York

An Imprint of Sterling Publishing Co., Inc.
1166 Avenue of the Americas
New York, NY 10036

Originally published as *Wicca Book of Spells* in 2016 by Wicca Shorts

This publication includes alternative therapies that have not been scientifically tested,
is intended for informational purposes only, and is not intended to provide or replace
conventional medical advice, treatment or diagnosis or be a substitute to consulting
with licensed medical or health-care providers. The publisher does not claim or
guarantee any benefits, healing, cure or any results in any respect and shall not be
liable or responsible for any use or application of any content in this publication in any
respect including without limitation any adverse effects, consequence, loss or damage
of any type resulting or arising from, directly or indirectly, any use or application of
any content herein. Any trademarks are the property of their respective owners, are
used for editorial purposes only, and the publisher makes no claim of ownership and
shall acquire no right, title or interest in such trademarks by virtue of this publication.

ISBN 978-1-4549-4082-1

Distributed in Canada by Sterling Publishing Co., Inc.
c/o Canadian Manda Group, 664 Annette Street
Toronto, Ontario, Canada M6S 2C8
Distributed in the United Kingdom by GMC Distribution Services
Castle Place, 166 High Street, Lewes, East Sussex, England BN7 1XU
Distributed in Australia by NewSouth Books
University of New South Wales, Sydney, NSW 2052, Australia

For information about custom editions, special sales, and premium and corporate
purchases, please contact Sterling Special Sales at 800-805-5489
or specialsales@sterlingpublishing.com.

Manufactured in Canada

6 8 10 9 7 5

sterlingpublishing.com

Design by Sharon Jacobs
Cover by Elizabeth M. Lindy
Picture credits—see page 129

FOR MAIRGHREAD

*—here's to the rest
of the story.*

CONTENTS

PART FOUR

ASSORTED SPELLS & STRATEGIES

INTRODUCTION

The world of magic is full of immeasurable potential. There are literally thousands of spells in existence, for every purpose you could possibly imagine. Of course, those who use magic as part of their practice of Wicca—and many other traditions of Witchcraft—will only work for positive or neutral purposes, *never seeking to harm anyone or anything*, and the spells in this book abide by this important rule.

In these pages you will find spells and other workings that, when applied with focused intention, can bring positive experiences into your life—and by extension, the lives of those you care about.

These spells cover a wide range of magical aims. Most are grouped into three categories: love and relationships, prosperity and abundance, and health and well-being, as these are the top three areas in life for which people tend to seek magical assistance.

However, they're not the only elements of the human experience, and that's why you'll find a sampling of other spells to give you just a hint of the possibilities for broadening your own magical practice.

In addition, this book covers a variety of magical approaches and techniques, from candle magic to divination to charms and other hand-made creations. Each spell contains explicit instructions, but there are also opportunities to personalize many of the workings as you see fit.

If you're already fairly experienced in magic, you'll probably know first-hand that you can generally make substitutions for ingredients that are hard to acquire. If you're new, it's often helpful to follow spells as closely to the letter as you can until you cultivate a stronger connection to your intuition for improvising, but if your inner wisdom guides you to do something differently, by all means listen to it!

Of course, as flexible as magic can be, there are certainly some key steps and considerations that go into successful spellwork.

First and foremost, please note that the instructions for each of these spells assume that you have already charged your ingredients for the magical purpose you are pursuing.

Methods for charging tend to vary according to the type of object you're working with, but if you're not sure how to proceed, you can use a standard method that works for most anything: lay the object on an already-charged pentacle, preferably in direct sunlight or moonlight, and speak words of intention related to the spellwork you'll be doing. Depending on your practice, you might invoke the Goddess and God, the Elements, or other spiritual energies you work with.

If you're new to magic, research and try a few different methods for charging various tools, until you find what feels most appropriate for you.

Second, always remember that no matter the kind or quality of your ingredients, how well you charge them, or how well you follow the spell instructions to the letter, it is your state of mind that is the chief factor in any successful spellwork.

Approach a spell with doubt that it will work, and you've pretty much guaranteed that it won't. Approach it with anxiety, and you're likely to get mixed results or no results at all.

The most successful magic is done from a place of calm centeredness and with very focused intent. So always do whatever you need to do to get grounded, whether that's through meditation, visualization, breathing techniques, a ritual circle-casting, or all of the above. It is ultimately *your* energy that's shifting the reality of the Universe, so shape it well and use it wisely!

One way to help ensure that your energetic focus is aligned with a spell is to rewrite the spoken element in your own words.

Of course, the words provided in these spells are already powerful and effective, but if you're inclined to be creative with language, you are invited to use words of your own.

Some Witches maintain that spells should rhyme, and there is definitely something to be said for the power that rhyme can lend to magic. Others find, however, that if a spell is too "sing-songy" it distracts them from speaking the words with authenticity and focus.

You'll find that some spells in this book make use of rhyme, while others do not. Try out some of each and see how you respond internally to the words, and again, feel free to tweak or completely rewrite them as you see fit.

A few more practical tips are worth mentioning here. Always work spells in a place where you know you'll be undisturbed by other people. Turn off your phone and do your best to create an ambience conducive to magic—whether that means music, incense, candles, and so on.

Speaking of candles, always use caution, and *never leave a burning candle unattended*. If you're anointing a candle with oil, be sure to wipe excess oil from your fingertips before sparking that match or lighter—you don't want to mix skin and oil with fire!

Also, when it comes to spells containing herbs, keep in mind that the amounts listed are general suggestions—there's no need to measure out *exact* teaspoons or tablespoons, unless you find that doing so adds energy and focus to the spell. Otherwise, a rough estimation of the listed amount will do—as always, go with your gut instinct!

Finally, no matter how much, or how little, experience you have with spellwork, remember that there is always more room to learn and grow. Enjoy trying out these magical offerings, and if you wish, let them be a springboard of inspiration for creating your own spells. And don't forget to honor your results with love and gratitude.

Blessed Be.

PART ONE

LOVE & RELATIONSHIP SPELLS

INTRODUCTION TO
LOVE & RELATIONSHIP
SPELLS

OF ALL THE REASONS PEOPLE TURN TO MAGIC, LOVE MAY BE the single most common. Since time immemorial, hopeful lovers have tried spells and potions of all sorts in order to bring them their one true love. This section certainly contains spells for attracting romantic love into your life, but it also includes workings related to friendship and family relationships, which are equally important sources of love in a balanced life. There's also a spell aimed at strengthening and solidifying your most important relationship—the one between you and your spiritual source.

As mentioned in the introduction, this spell book works with positive magic only. This means you won't find any spells in this section that will cause someone to act or feel toward you in a way that could be contradictory to their free will. Such spells are almost guaranteed to backfire, and even if they do work for a time, you'll always know that you manipulated the person in question, which doesn't make for a genuine relationship.

So commit instead to directing your magical energy for the highest good of all involved in whatever your situation may be. You'll attract connections of a much higher quality that way, and feel better about yourself and your life as a result.

SPELL FOR
NEW FRIENDSHIPS

Whether you've just moved to a new area and don't know many people yet, or your social life simply needs an overhaul, this quick spell brings new people into your life to form friendships with if you so choose.

It's best done during a waxing moon, but if you've got an upcoming social encounter that you'd like to put some magical energy into, by all means don't hold off just because the moon is waning.

≡ YOU WILL NEED ≡

**1 small rose quartz, clear quartz, carnelian,
or lapis lazuli stone**

1 yellow spell or votive candle

Lavender essential oil

+ Anoint the candle with the oil.

+ Place the stone in your dominant hand, palm upward, and lay your other palm on top.

+ Clasp your hands together, close your eyes, and visualize yourself surrounded by positive people who are fun and comforting to be around.

+ When you've captured this feeling, take a deep breath, exhale, and open your eyes.

+ Place the stone in front of the candle and then light the wick as you say these words:

> *"Friendships new and true,*
> *let our kindred souls unite."*

+ Carry the stone with you whenever you leave the house, and leave it where you will see it when you are home.

RELATIONSHIP STRENGTHENING SPELL

When the "honeymoon phase" of a new relationship inevitably begins to fade, it's common for one or both partners to experience doubts or grapple with unresolved emotional blocks from the past. The ability to work through these issues with open hearts and mutual respect is what strengthens the bond between two people. Ultimately, a healthy relationship offers opportunities for both partners to learn from each other and grow as human beings.

This spell is a wonderful way to sow the seeds of harmony and good faith as your relationship deepens. It can be worked by you alone, or with your partner if they'd like to participate.

In the Tarot, the card known as "The Lovers" represents romantic love, as well as partnerships, growth, loyalty, and choices. It makes a perfect focal point for this spell, as you are declaring your intent to show up for yourself and your partner when challenges arise. There are many variations of this card across different Tarot decks. For best results, use one with imagery that pleases you.

≡ YOU WILL NEED ≡

- 1 work candle for atmosphere
- 1 pink spell candle
- 1 Lovers Tarot card
- 2 pieces rose quartz, lapis lazuli, moonstone, or aventurine (use two of the same type)
- ¼ teaspoon fresh or dried rosemary
- ¼ teaspoon fresh or dried lavender
- ¼ teaspoon dried hibiscus petals
- ¼ teaspoon dried chamomile flowers
- 1 small bowl
- Cinnamon, juniper, rose, or love-related anointing oil

+ Light the work candle.

+ Mix the herbs gently in the bowl with your fingers, visualizing your energy flowing into each leaf, petal, and flower.

+ Place the Lovers card face-up in the center of your altar.

+ Anoint the spell candle with the oil and place it several inches behind the card.

+ Spend some time taking in the imagery of the card. Then hold one crystal in each open palm as you summon the feeling of being in harmony and open communication with your partner. When you feel ready, place a crystal next to each side of the card, aligning it as close as possible to the heart of the figure on that side.

+ Now sprinkle the herbs in a circle around the card and the crystals as you say the following (or similar) words:

"I open my heart to love.
I honor my soul's wish to grow.
I am present with my partner,
listening with my heart,
as we walk this path together.
And so it is."

+ Light the spell candle and leave it to burn out on its own. Leave the work on your altar for 24 hours.

+ Carry the crystals with you and/or place them in a prominent place in your home. If your partner is participating and doesn't live with you, they should keep one of the crystals with them.

CHARM FOR ATTRACTING QUALITY RELATIONSHIPS

As a culinary spice, coriander has a warm, fragrant, slightly nutty flavor. But not everyone knows that coriander is actually the seed of the herb known as cilantro. Interestingly, the seed and the leaf taste nothing alike. This dual nature is reflected in the magical uses of coriander, which include both attracting love and guarding against unwanted energies.

The seed is used in love spells, aphrodisiac potions, and for making peace between quarreling people, as well as for exorcism and protection of the home. And because it's readily available in the spice aisle of most grocery stores, it's a great herb to work with for beginning kitchen Witches.

This spell draws on both the attracting and protective qualities of coriander for a balanced approach to attracting new potential partners into your life.

This is particularly good for those who seem to have no trouble attracting admirers, but plenty of trouble in the relationships that develop. With the energy of coriander, people who are ultimately no good for you will not make it into your sphere of awareness, while people who present a positive, healthy, compatible match will have a clear path to you.

Adding rose quartz to the mix enhances the positive vibration of the spell. Be sure to get whole seeds rather than coriander powder, since you'll be carrying the herb with you.

≡ YOU WILL NEED ≡

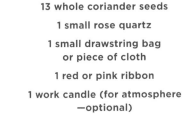

13 whole coriander seeds

1 small rose quartz

1 small drawstring bag
or piece of cloth

1 red or pink ribbon

1 work candle (for atmosphere
—optional)

≡ INSTRUCTIONS ≡

+ Light the candle, if using.

+ Arrange the coriander seeds in a circle around the rose quartz.

+ Close your eyes and visualize the feeling of being completely at peace with a partner who loves you for exactly who you are.

+ When you have a lock on this feeling, open your eyes, focus on the rose quartz, and say the following (or similar) words:

*"I draw to me nothing less than
healthy, balanced love."*

+ Now collect the coriander seeds, placing them one at a time into the drawstring bag or cloth. (It's best to start with the seed at the southernmost part of the circle and move clockwise.)

+ Add the rose quartz, close the bag or cloth, and secure with the ribbon.

+ Bring the charm with you whenever you're feeling like taking a chance on love—especially when you go out in public.

ROMANCE
ATTRACTION
SMUDGE

This is a fun, simple ritual for enhancing the atmosphere in your home, or any space where you'd like to encourage romance!

Rose oil adds a nice magical boost, but don't feel the need to purchase it just for this spell (though if you enjoy roses, this can be a very nice oil to have on hand generally).

Be sure not to use a blended smudge stick, such as one with sage and lavender or cedar and lavender—these are great for other purposes, but in this case they will dilute the romantic vibrations of the lavender.

1 red candle

**Sprig of dried lavender or
lavender-only smudge stick**

**Rose essential oil
(optional)**

1 feather (optional)

≡ INSTRUCTIONS ≡

+ Anoint the candle with a drop or two of the rose oil, if using. Wipe away any excess oil from your fingers, and then light the candle.

+ Ignite the lavender sprig or smudge stick from the candle flame as you say the following (or similar) words:

*"Loving lavender, creative fire,
charge this space with love's desire."*

+ Starting at a point in the northern part in the room, move in a clockwise circle, fanning the lavender smoke with the feather (if using) or your hand, so that it spreads throughout the room as much as possible. If you like, you can repeat the words of power above as a chant as you go.

+ Leave the lavender to burn out on its own in a heat-resistant dish, if possible—otherwise, you can extinguish it gently in a potted plant or bowl of sand.

STELLAR FIRST DATE
CONFIDENCE
CHARM

If you're the type who gets nervous before meeting a potential love interest for the first time, this spell is for you.

Simply carry the charm with you in your pocket or purse—you may want to enclose it in a drawstring bag or cloth if you're carrying it with other items to keep it intact.

Keep in mind that the focus here is on your own confidence and sense of self-love *no matter what the other person is like*. If you have a good time, no matter what the outcome, then the spell has been a success.

YOU WILL NEED

1 white or pink ribbon,
about 7 inches in length

1 small piece of carnelian
or tiger's eye

Sea salt

1 work candle (for atmosphere
—optional)

1 small drawstring bag
or piece of cloth
(optional)

- ✦ Light the candle, if using.
- ✦ Lay out the ribbon on your altar or work space.
- ✦ Create a circle of sea salt around the ribbon—this will concentrate the energy of the spell around the charm.
- ✦ Place the stone on the ribbon, and say the following (or similar) words:

> *"My confidence radiates from within*
> *I am comfortable in my own skin*
> *This meeting of souls will be a pleasure*
> *I charm this stone for extra measure."*

- ✦ Tie the ribbon gently around the stone and secure with a knot.
- ✦ Now go out and have fun meeting someone new!

RITUAL BATH FOR
A BLIND DATE

Whether you're on a blind date set up by a friend, or taking the plunge in the world of online dating, it can be nerve-wracking to meet someone new.

This spell makes it nearly impossible not to have a good time, by sublimating nervousness and promoting self-confidence, which will improve the energy of the encounter no matter what the outcome. Indeed, you will enjoy yourself even if it's clear by the end that there won't be a second date!

Himalayan salt is a wonderful relaxant, but it can be potent and induce sleepiness, especially if you don't use it regularly. Therefore, if you're taking this bath right before the date, you may want to opt for the sea salt.

The herbs can be sprinkled loosely if you have a mesh catchall drain for your tub. Otherwise, place them in a tea bag or a thin washcloth to keep them from spreading out into the water.

1 teaspoon to 1 tablespoon hibiscus

1 teaspoon to 1 tablespoon chamomile

1 teaspoon to 1 tablespoon coltsfoot or red clover

2–3 tablespoons sea salt or Himalayan salt

5 drops lavender essential oil

1 piece citrine, aventurine, or tiger's eye

Candle(s) for atmosphere

≡ INSTRUCTIONS ≡

+ Run the bath until the tub is a quarter of the way full, and add the salt.

+ When the tub is halfway full, place the crystal of your choice in the water, and add the oil.

+ When the bath is almost full, add the herbs.

+ Light the candle(s), turn off any artificial lighting in the bathroom, and climb in.

+ Relax and consciously release any anxiety you may be feeling about meeting this new person. Also release any attachments you may be feeling to a desired outcome.

+ Stay in the bath for at least 20 minutes. If you can, remain in the tub while draining the water, as the energy of the herbs and crystal tends to have a stronger effect that way.

+ Bring the crystal with you on the date, and have a good time!

WILLOW SPELL
FOR LETTING GO
OF LOVE

The end of a relationship, whether by mutual agreement or by one person's choice, results in an experience of grief. Even in the best of situations, there are still losses to process and adjust to: the loss of companionship, familiar routines, emotional and physical intimacy.

Often, the desire (or well-meaning advice) to "get over it" is really the desire to evade this part of the process of moving on. This ritual provides a structure for actively acknowledging and releasing the feelings of grief, rather than trying to suppress or hold on to them.

The willow tree has long been known for its healing energies, helping soothe both physical and emotional pain. If you don't live near any willows, try working with an ash, birch, fir, or oak tree, or any tree you feel drawn to.

≡ YOU WILL NEED ≡

Willow (or other) tree

Journal or writing paper

Small slip of paper

Small spade (or spoon)

≡ INSTRUCTIONS ≡

+ Sit as near to the trunk of the tree as you can. Bring a chair if sitting on the ground is a challenge for you.

+ Write the name of the person you're letting go of on the small slip of paper and place it at the base of the trunk.

+ Now write a "goodbye" letter to the person. You won't be sending it to them, so you can express yourself freely, but make the letter as positive as you can.

+ Express appreciation for their positive qualities and the good times you spent together. You can also acknowledge your sadness, of course, but avoid wandering into unresolved arguments or resentments. This is about letting go of what you would have wished to keep, rather than focusing on what you won't miss about the relationship.

+ When you're finished, read the letter out loud. Then use the spade to bury the small slip of paper near the base of the tree.

+ Walk away and don't look back. The letter can be burned, or torn into small pieces and recycled.

APPLE PENTAGRAM
DIVINATION
SPELL

Apple trees are considered sacred to Witches for several reasons, not least of which is the pentagram shape of the seeds in the center of the fruit.

Apples are used in a variety of magical workings, including peeling the apple in one spiraling slice and dropping it to the floor to see the first letter of your true love's name.

The divination technique below relies on the appearance of the pentagram after the apple is sliced in half. It can be used for any question at any time, but is particularly good for matters of romance and during the Autumn harvest season.

Be sure to eat the apple or compost it afterward—don't let this magical fruit go to waste!

1 apple

A boline or other slicing knife

1 black, white, or pink candle
(optional)

≡ INSTRUCTIONS ≡

✦ Light the candle, if using.

✦ Spend some time getting clear on your question, holding
the apple in your hand.

✦ Assign one possible answer to the top half of the apple and
the other to the bottom half (the best questions for this
are yes or no questions).

✦ Slice the apple in half horizontally so the pentagram pattern
of the seed pockets is revealed.

✦ If the seeds are all in one half of the apple, then you have your
answer. If the seeds are split between the two halves or fall out,
there is not enough information yet for a clear answer.

✦ Save the seeds & either plant them or scatter them in a
beautiful place in nature, silently giving thanks for the answer,
no matter what it may be.

SPELL TO RELEASE
NEGATIVE ATTACHMENTS

At some point or other, everyone experiences a nagging conflict that can't be immediately resolved through conversation. Whether it's with an ex-lover, a difficult coworker, or a family member, some situations just need time and distance before peace can be achieved.

In the meantime, it can be difficult to refrain from obsessing over the details and remaining in the negative energy that the conflict has created. This spell helps you to detach from the situation, regardless of how the other person is behaving. Note that the focus here is on you and your own energy, and not on the other person! The point is to disengage from the conflict so you can be at peace no matter how long it takes to resolve the situation.

This is ideally worked during a waning moon, but if the situation is really troubling you, do not wait until you are even further entrenched in the negativity—go ahead, release the attachment!

YOU WILL NEED

1 black candle

1 strip of paper (about
1 × 7 inches [2.5 × 17.8 cm])

Journal or additional
paper (optional)

1 pen or pencil

Small cauldron or
heat-resistant dish

Frankincense, sandalwood,
or sage incense

+ Light the incense.

+ For best results, spend at least 10 to 15 minutes freewriting about the conflict and the feelings you're having a hard time letting go of. Don't indulge or dwell on negative thinking here, but rather see this activity as a sort of psychic "exorcism" in which you remove the thoughts and emotions from your mind once and for all.

+ When you feel you've achieved this, take the piece of paper you're using in the spell and write down the name of the person and a brief (one-sentence maximum) summary of the conflict.

+ Roll the paper into a loose scroll.

+ Light the candle, take a few deep breaths, and say the following (or similar) words:

> *"With this candle, on this night,*
> *I let go of my attachments to being right.*
>
> *In the space left by this release,*
> *My being is filled with healing peace."*

+ Ignite the scroll of paper with the candle flame, and let it burn completely in the cauldron or dish.

+ When the ashes are cooled, gently toss them out onto the Earth.

+ For best results, leave the candle to burn out on its own.

+ In the days that follow, if you find yourself returning to thoughts of the conflict, remember your spellwork, take a deep breath, and visualize the ashes of the negativity disappearing into the soil of the Earth.

CHOOSING PEACE IN TOUGH SITUATIONS

At some point in our lives, we all face enormous challenges that we know we can do nothing to control. It may be that a loved one is facing a serious illness, or it may even be a major world event causing chaos in your life.

It's always fine to work magic for whatever influence you may be able to have on the outcome of a situation, but this can be difficult to do from a place of empowerment when you're feeling personally affected, which can negate the energy of the spell. In times like these, you need to take care of yourself first before you can help anyone else.

The soothing properties of lavender, chamomile, and ylang-ylang in the Peace of Mind Oil blend (see page 107) put you in touch with your core self and your connection to spirit, to help you let go of the situation—at least for a time—and regain your inner balance.

This spell is best worked an hour or so before going to bed. If you prefer to let spell candles burn all the way down on their own, you'll need to place it in a sink before going to sleep! Otherwise, you can gently extinguish the candle and repeat the spell on successive nights until the candle is spent.

This spell is really meant to be personalized as much as you wish. Put on meditative music, brew chamomile tea, stretch your limbs, take a hot bath, and/or do anything else that helps you relax. The more energetically "prepped" you are for this spell, the more powerful it will be.

**Peace of Mind Oil blend
(see page 106)**

1 white candle

**Meditative music
(optional)**

≡ INSTRUCTIONS ≡

+ Put on the music, if using, and take any other measures to calm yourself as much as you can.

+ Sit quietly and take a few deep breaths. Anoint your pulse points and the candle with the oil.

+ Close your eyes and take a few more deep breaths, clearing your mind as much as possible.

+ When you feel ready, open your eyes and light the candle, while saying the following (or similar) words:

> *"I release this burden to
> my higher power
> and turn my attention to
> balance and rest.
> So let it be."*

+ Sit and gaze at the candle flame for several moments, keeping your mind as quiet as possible and your focus on the light.

"SPARE KEY" SPELL FOR SPIRITUAL CONNECTION

Although we usually think of other people in the context of "relationship," we also have a relationship with our "higher power"—or whatever your personal term is for the force that moves through you when working magic. This spell focuses on strengthening that relationship, which is ultimately the foundation from which all human relationships stem.

While it may be becoming less common in today's world, it has long been the custom of many households to keep a spare key just outside the home, whether under the doormat, in a potted plant, or in some other hidden location. This is done as both a backup in the case of lost keys, and as a way of allowing relatives or friends access when the homeowner is away.

This spell draws on the energies of wisdom and trust that are inherent to this custom, as a way of honoring the benevolent forces working for you in the unseen realms.

By blessing and burying a key outside near your home (or in a potted plant indoors, if necessary) you are signaling to your higher power—whether it be a deity, a guardian spirit, or simply the benevolent energy of the Universe—that you welcome their presence and assistance in your home and in your life, no matter where you may be at any given moment.

It is also a way of reminding yourself that should you temporarily lose your connection to your spiritual center, you will always be able to find your way back in.

Depending on whether crime is a factor in your neighborhood, you may feel comfortable using an actual spare key to your home, but any metal key will work for this spell.

Some people like to use a gold key to represent the God and/or a silver key to represent the Goddess (using two keys is also fine).

=== **YOU WILL NEED** ===

1 key

1 white candle

=== **INSTRUCTIONS** ===

+ Hold the key in your hands while meditating quietly for several minutes. Focus on that feeling of being truly connected to your true self and your higher power.

+ When you feel ready, light the candle and say the following (or similar) words:

> "[name of deity/spirit/higher power],
> *you are welcome now and always*
> *in my home and in my heart.*
>
> *Let this key represent your access, and mine,*
> *to my highest self, from this day forward."*

+ Pass the key through the candle flame very quickly three times (in order to protect your fingers, don't give it any time to become hot).

+ Then bury it at least 6 inches down into the earth outside your home, or in the soil of a large potted plant.

THREE-HERBS
LOVE CHARM

The magical properties of lavender, hibiscus, and basil all include love. This spell can be for attracting new love or renewing love in an existing relationship, but either way, be sure you're focusing on how you want to feel, and not on controlling the feelings or behavior of another person.

≡ YOU WILL NEED ≡

Dried lavender

Dried hibiscus

Dried basil

1 small rose quartz crystal

Small square of white, pink,
red, or violet soft cloth
(silk or velvet
is ideal)

A length of white, pink,
red, or violet
ribbon

+ Hold the rose quartz in your hands and charge it with loving vibrations by meditating on how you want to feel when your goal is manifested.

+ Lay out the cloth and gently lay the crystal on it.

+ Sprinkle a pinch of each of the herbs onto the crystal.

+ As you sprinkle each herb, name it and affirm its purpose. You might say:

"With this lavender
I manifest love in my life."

+ Fold the cloth over the rose quartz and wrap it gently until you can tie the ribbon around the charm.

+ Carry it with you in your purse or pocket and/or put it under your pillow at night.

PART TWO

WEALTH & PROSPERITY SPELLS

INTRODUCTION TO WEALTH & PROSPERITY SPELLS

THE SECOND MOST FREQUENT REASON FOR WORKING WITH magic is almost certainly the need or desire for money. While most people realize that manifesting a multimillion-dollar lottery win from a simple candle spell is generally unlikely to happen, we know that we can attract money from unforeseen places into our lives through the use of focused intention. This section contains a handful of fun spells to try doing just that!

However, "cold hard cash" is not the only form of wealth available to us, and it's important to acknowledge other avenues of abundance and prosperity for a well-rounded life.

Opportunities for growing future wealth are also important, for example, as are an abundance of friends, pleasurable activities, and healthy options for nourishing our bodies. To that end, you'll also find spells for increasing business success, abundance in the garden, and even a spell for landing an important job.

So enjoy the thrill of experiencing an unexpected windfall, but don't lose sight of the bigger picture of truly prosperous living.

GARDEN
PLANTING SPELL

Whether you're planning a full-fledged flower or vegetable garden, or just a few indoor potted plants, this spell can lend a magical boost to the start of the growing season. It's best to work this spell immediately before planting your seeds or plant starts, so the energy is fresh and strong when they go into the soil.

If you're just planting one type of seed, try emptying the seed packet into the bowl to charge them directly. If you're charging multiple types of seeds together, however, you may want to keep them in their packets.

If using plant starts, you'll probably need to charge each individually, unless you have a fairly large-size bowl. Keep them in their containers for the spell and then transplant them to the soil afterward.

Seeds or plant starts (seedlings)

**Ceramic, stone, glass, or wooden bowl
(anything but plastic will do)**

≡ INSTRUCTIONS ≡

+ Hold the bowl in your hands, close your eyes, and visualize your own loving and powerful energy flowing into the bowl and then into the seeds/plant starts.

+ When you can feel a strong, consistent flow of energy, say the following (or similar) words:

> *"Force of life that flows through all
> hear now this gardener's call.*
>
> *These living seeds I hereby nourish
> with the energy they need to flourish."*

+ Now, plant your seeds and watch them grow. (Don't forget to water them, of course!)

MOONLIGHT PROSPERITY SPELL

Coins make for good magical tools for prosperity, not only because they are literal representations of wealth, but because they can also symbolize the seeds of future wealth to come.

The ideal time for this spell is at the Full Moon, but it can be worked on any night when the moon is waxing and moonlight is accessible—either outdoors or through a window.

⟹ YOU WILL NEED ⟸

3 silver coins

Small cauldron, or glass or ceramic bowl

Water

1 white, green, gold or silver candle

1 soft piece of cloth

1 small drawstring bag or second piece of cloth

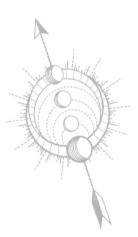

+ Place the coins in the cauldron or bowl and fill it about two-thirds full with water.

+ Leave the bowl in direct moonlight for at least one hour to charge the coins.

+ When you're ready to work the spell, bring the cauldron or bowl to your altar or work space, and light the candle.

+ Wave your hands (or your wand, if you use one) gently over the bowl while saying the following (or similar) words:

"Goddess of Moon, shine
your infinite light. Let limitless
wealth be my fortune this night.

Boundless as water, let
abundance flow.
These coins are the seeds from
which my wealth grows."

+ Remove the coins from the water and dry them gently with the cloth.

+ Place them in the drawstring bag (or fold in the second piece of cloth) and leave them next to the burning candle for at least an hour (or until the candle burns down).

+ Pour the water out onto the ground outside your house. (If this is not possible for some reason, pour it into a dry potted plant.)

+ Carry the coin bundle in your pocket or purse for the next seven days.

CALLING IN THE CASH

Wealth can come into our lives in many different forms, but it can be fun to work magic that focuses specifically on physical money. Watch for the interesting ways in which coins and bills suddenly manifest in the weeks after you work this spell!

The Wealth Attraction Oil is the key ingredient, as it connects you physically and psychically to the two other items involved—the candle and the cash. Think of it as the magical signal that is calling more physical money into your experience.

And if you're using your own handmade oil blend by following the Wealth Attraction Oil recipe (see page 106), then it will be even more powerful! (If you have a comparable store-bought blend, however, feel free to work this spell with it.)

As for the paper bill, it's ideal to use as large a denomination as possible, as this raises the bar, energetically, on what you're calling in. But don't feel discouraged if a smaller bill is all you can spare at this time. You can always work the spell again with a bigger bill down the road!

In regard to the candle, gold can sometimes be a difficult color to come by, so feel free to use a green one if need be. If this is the case, however, you might want to supplement the spell by arranging some gold-colored objects around your altar or work space, such as pyrite or other golden-hued crystals, jewelry, or gold coins.

1 gold (or green) spell or votive candle

Wealth Attraction Oil
(see page 106)

A $1, $5, $10, or $20 bill
(or higher, depending on how comfortable
you feel carrying cash with you)

1 green or gold ribbon

=== INSTRUCTIONS ===

+ First, anoint your temples, third eye, and pulse points with the oil. Then anoint the candle, starting at the base and working your way up to the top.

+ Anoint the bill at each corner on both sides. Then fold the bill into a triangle shape, and bind with the ribbon.

+ Light the candle, and tilt it over the center of the folded bill so that a little wax drips onto the ribbon.

+ Place the candle in its holder, and when the wax on the bill has dried a bit, place the bill gently between your palms.

+ Say the following (or similar words) three times:

> *"Essence of abundance, I call you forth into*
> *my life in the form of solid currency."*

+ Leave candle to burn out on its own. Carry the magically charged bill with you in your wallet for at least 1 month.

ABUNDANT HOME FLOOR WASH

Cleaning chores can become magical moments when you take the right approach. Add some magical oils and your own powerful energy to a few basic ingredients, and then welcome the flow of abundance into your home.

Patchouli, bergamot, cedarwood, and vetiver oil are associated with prosperity and abundance, and work well in cleaning products. Lemon oil brings a bright, refreshing energy into the mix for a boosting effect. This solution is safe on hard wood floors and tile.

It's ideal to do this with a brand-new mop, so that the mop's very first use is an intentionally magical one. A microfiber mop pad is best. But it's fine if you have a perfectly good mop already. The main thing is to make sure the mop head you're using is quite clean before you start.

≡ YOU WILL NEED ≡

- 1 work candle (optional)
- 1 teaspoon castile soap (Dr. Bronner's works well)
- 4 cups warm water
- Spray bottle

- 10–15 drops patchouli, bergamot, cedarwood, and/or vetiver oil
- 2–3 drops lemon oil (optional)
- Mop

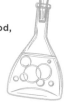

+ Light the candle, if using.
+ Combine the soap and water in a spray bottle and shake vigorously to mix.
+ Add a few drops of oil, visualizing the bright energy of abundance throughout your home.
+ Test the overall scent of the mixture before adding more.
+ Repeat this process for each different oil.
+ Close the bottle and swirl the mixture around three times in a sunwise (clockwise) motion and say the following (or similar) words:

"Out with the old, in with the new.
This potent potion makes it true.

Soon my floor(s) will
gleam and shine,
and true abundance will be mine."

+ As you clean, listen to upbeat music you love and feel free to dance and sing.
+ When you're finished, take time to appreciate the satisfaction of a job well done.
+ Variation: if you prefer an old-fashioned mop and bucket session, you can increase the amount of castile soap and water, or even substitute Murphy's or other natural floor cleaner.

PYRITE FOR PROSPERITY CHANGE JAR

One of the most sparkling crystals in the mineral kingdom is pyrite, with its cube-shaped formations glittering all over the surface of each stone. It also has quite powerful energy, which makes it a good "beginner" stone for those learning to increase their physical sensitivity to crystals. Hold one in your palm, and you may be surprised by its weight relative to other stones as well as its almost "buzzing" energy.

Pyrite is used for many magical aims, including balance, boosting self-confidence, and stimulating wealth. It's a stone uniquely suited to help create a harmonious interweaving of the creative/intuitive part of ourselves with our logical/rational aspects, both of which are necessary for a successful life.

Pyrite is also known as "fool's gold" because inexperienced miners would often mistake it for the real thing. This may seem ironic for a stone used in prosperity spells, but it makes sense when you realize that pyrite's magic emphasizes a creative and logical approach to wealth, rather than mere luck.

This spell works by connecting the physical energy of pyrite to actual money, which will flow in and out of the jar, integrating the spellwork into your daily life. You can use just about any container, but be sure to make it an attractive one that will raise your personal energetic vibration when you look at it. Some people might go out and buy an attractive jar or bowl for this purpose, while others like to decorate a plain jar, which adds extra magical energy to the endeavor.

1 medium-sized raw pyrite stone

Jar for keeping change

Several coins of different denominations

Decorating materials
(optional)

≡ INSTRUCTIONS ≡

+ If you're decorating your jar, it's nice to do this as the first step of the spellwork, but you can do it ahead of time if need be.

+ When you're ready to start, charge the pyrite by holding it between your palms for several moments, focusing on the feeling of balance and prosperity.

+ When you can feel a strong energy running through your hands, say the following (or similar) words:

"In wealth and wisdom,
my life grows."

+ Place the pyrite at the bottom of the jar, and gently drop in the coins.

+ Whenever you add coins or remove them from the jar, acknowledge the pyrite in some way—either by thanking it, or by repeating the words of the spell.

+ Be sure to also honor your own capacity for creatively influencing your financial life.

CINNAMON
MONEY MAGNET CHARM

Best known as a distinctive spice, usually in its powdered form, cinnamon is also used in spells for prosperity and luck. It is traditionally added to some magical workings to add "heat" to the energy of the other ingredients, boosting their power and speeding up the manifestation time.

Here, cinnamon is used in stick form as a powerful magical item all on its own. Its scent makes this an ideal charm to place in your car, but you can also hang it in your kitchen, or any place where you'll see it often.

Most cinnamon sticks have a hollow center. Be sure to choose one that can be threaded with a ribbon or length of yarn. Ribbon can make for a more attractive, long-lasting charm, but anything that's wide enough to stay threaded through the stick without slipping out will work.

1 cinnamon stick,
2–3 inches in length

1 green or gold ribbon, 12–18 inches
(30.5–45.7 cm) in length

≡ INSTRUCTIONS ≡

+ Thread the ribbon through the hollow of the cinnamon stick
  and tie the ends securely.

+ Hold the stick in both palms and close your eyes. Imagine
  a storm of dollar bills flying at you from all directions.

+ Gently touch the stick to the pulse points at your wrists,
  elbows, neck, and temples as you say the following (or similar)
  words:

"Sweet wood of cinnamon,
draw to me my fortune.

In record time, more money is mine,
attracted with this talisman."

+ Hang your "money magnet" somewhere visible and try to
  touch it at least once every day.

JOB INTERVIEW SUCCESS SPELL

Help counteract the anxiety of an important interview and increase your chance of success. This spell is ideal when the moon is waxing to full, but don't let that stop you if the interview takes place between the Full and New Moon!

1 orange or gold candle

Incense (frankincense, lilac, or cinnamon)

Pen/pencil and piece of paper

1 small piece of lapis lazuli, citrine, or tiger's eye

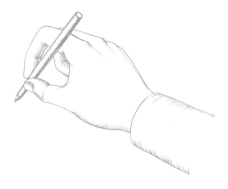

- Light the incense, and anoint the candle with the oil.
- Spend a few moments visualizing yourself feeling calm and confident at the interview.
- On the paper, write down three reasons why you are the best candidate for the position.
- Fold the paper into a triangle no bigger than a few inches and place it in front of the candle.
- Light the candle, saying the following (or similar) words:

> *"In perfect place*
> *and perfect time as*
> *I light this candle,*
> *the job is mine."*

- Pass the crystal quickly through the candle flame, then set it on top of the paper.
- Leave the candle to burn out safely on its own.
- Bring the folded paper and the crystal to the interview.
- Once you land the job, tear the paper into small pieces and recycle it. Be sure to thank your powers that be, but also congratulate yourself for a solid interview!

POTTED CHARM
FOR SUCCESSFUL BUSINESS

Whether you're just starting a business or want to boost the success of an existing one, a simple potted plant can do wonders. It's also a highly discreet piece of ongoing magic—your customers won't have a clue that your "lucky charm" is anything other than a plant!

Bamboo and aloe are two popular plants that are associated with good luck, and both are easy to grow indoors. If your business has outdoor garden space, lavender and basil are excellent prosperity plants. Choose one or more plants that both appeal to you personally and feel like the right choice for your location.

≡ YOU WILL NEED ≡

**1 or more clay or ceramic pots
with adequate drainage**

**1 or more plant starts (seedlings)
of your choice**

1 dollar coin for each plant

Potting soil *

Water *

+ Pour a thin layer of soil at the base of the pot.

+ Place the dollar coin on the soil, press gently with your fingers, and say the following (or similar) words:

> *"My business is solid from its very foundation*
> *in this rich and fertile soil."*

+ Fill the pot with enough soil for potting the plant start, and create a space for the root ball to nestle into.

+ After you've gently secured the plant start in the soil and packed sufficient soil around it, water it thoroughly, saying the following (or similar) words:

> *"My business is rooted securely*
> *in growth and good fortune."*

+ Place the pot in its location in your business. With your palms on either side of the pot, say the following (or similar) words:

> *"My business enriches my life*
> *and the lives of others.*
> *My business is prosperous and beautiful."*

+ As you regularly tend to your plant(s), remember your spellwork and silently thank the plant(s) for contributing to the growing success of your business.

** The ideal soil type, as well as amounts of water
and sunlight, will vary between different types of plants.
For best results, follow the instructions recommended
for the plant(s) you're working with.

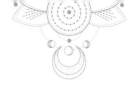

"BLANK CHECK"
PROSPERITY SPELL

A check is a banking instrument that represents the flow of money from one source to another. This spell creates a daily reminder of your power to manifest infinite abundance, and helps to dissolve entrenched patterns of limited thinking about money.

If you have a checkbook, choose a check with a number that has special significance for you. It may contain the numbers of your birthday, for example, or a number you associate with good luck. (If you don't have checks, you can request a counter check from your bank, go online and download a blank check template, or create one yourself.)

If you don't have a silver or gold marker, use a green or royal blue pen or colored pencil, or any special writing instrument you keep for spellwork.

To go the extra mile with this spell, frame the check after the candle has burned down. You can use a photo frame, make and decorate a frame of your own, or mat the check on some sturdy paper and brush it with Mod Podge®. Get creative and have fun!

=== YOU WILL NEED ===

1 green, royal blue, silver, or gold candle

1 blank check

Silver or gold marker/other writing instrument

Patchouli, clary sage, or cinnamon essential oil

Materials for matting/framing the check (optional)

+ Light the candle and spend some time conjuring a feeling of relaxed and confident abundance. Imagine you have everything on the material plane you could possibly need, access to everything you want, and the absolute knowledge that more will always be on the way. When you have a solid hold on this feeling, fill in the blanks on the check with the following:

    + Pay to the Order of: [*your name*]
    + Amount line: *"Unlimited Prosperity"*
    + Amount box: [*draw the infinity symbol*]
    + Date: *"Today and Every Day"*
    + Memo: *"I am Infinitely Abundant"*
    + Signature: *"The Universe"*

+ Over your name and address in the top left corner, draw a pentacle or another prosperity symbol of your choice.

+ Anoint the four corners of the check with a small bit of oil (try to avoid smearing any ink). Hold the check up in both hands and say the following (or similar) words:

"Today and every day, I am infinitely abundant.
I draw the unlimited energy of prosperity
into my life, for all time.
And so it is."

+ Place the check in front of the candle and leave it until the candle burns out on its own. Frame or mat it, if you choose to. Either way, place the check where you'll see it often.

NOTE: This spell can be tweaked to focus on debt elimination, which is often people's primary concern when it comes to finances. Simply write *"All Debt Resolved"* on the amount line instead, and visualize this outcome. Once your debts are paid off, you can burn the check or tear it into tiny pieces and recycle them.

HONEY ABUNDANCE JAR

The use of herbs and honey in a spell jar is widely practiced in the hoodoo tradition. These can be somewhat involved workings with several ingredients, but they have lasting effects and can be reused continually over long periods of time.

It's best to use local, unprocessed honey if you can find it, but commercial honey from the grocery store will also work just fine.

You can substitute the herbs below with any of your choosing, but be sure to go with herbs associated with money, abundance, and prosperity. For best results, you should use at least three herbs, but feel free to get more elaborate—the more the merrier!

The candles will be used one at a time, so you only need one to start with, but the idea is to keep the magic going over several weeks, so you'll want more to "feed" the spell with after the first one is spent.

1 small jar with screw-top lid

Honey (enough to fill the jar)

1 crystal/stone (lodestone/
   magnetite, citrine, green
   aventurine, pyrite, or
   tiger's eye)

8 sunflower seeds

3 or more green spell or
   taper candles

Mortar and pestle
(or bowl and spoon)

Patchouli oil for candle
(optional)

Crystal tip or pin (optional)

1–3 teaspoons of each
   (or at least three) of
   the following:

+ Lavender
+ Irish moss
+ Chamomile
+ Nutmeg
+ Alfalfa
+ Basil
+ Goldenseal
+ Chicory
+ Calamus roots

≡ INSTRUCTIONS ≡

+ Place all of the herbs in the mortar (or bowl) and mix them
  together with the pestle (or spoon).

+ Then use your fingers to mix them further, to infuse the herbs
  with your own personal energy (be sure to wash your hands
  before beginning this spell). As you do this, focus on your
  intention, whether it's money, some other form of abundance,
  or both.

+ Next, place the stone in the jar, focusing on its power to attract
  abundance into your life.

+ Cover the stone with the herbs, then sprinkle the sunflower
  seeds on top.

+ Pour the honey over the mixture until it reaches the top
  of the jar.

- Seal the jar with the lid and hold it in your hands for a few moments, visualizing the abundance flowing into your life.

- If you wish, inscribe the candle with a rune or other symbol representing your request, and anoint it with the patchouli oil.

- Then melt the bottom end of the candle with a lighter so it will stick to the lid of the jar. (Alternatively, you can light the candle and tilt it so a few drops of wax drip onto the lid, and affix the candle that way.)

- Leave the burning candle to go out on its own, and repeat this step weekly (or more often) as needed.

- Eventually you will sense that it's time to stop using the jar. When this time comes, thank it for its work.

- The traditional method for releasing this spell is to bury the jar in the ground. However, many contemporary practitioners will pour the contents out into the sink or compost, rinse and recycle the jar, and just bury the stone.

- If you go this route, be sure to release the spell as you open the jar. You can say something like:

"I thank these herbs and this honey
for the abundance that has manifested,
and release these energies back
to the Earth."

SPRING BLOSSOMS SPELL

Spring is such a magical time. From the first chirping of birds to the buds emerging on branches, evidence of new life seems to appear out of nowhere. Why not harness some of that growth-fueled energy by using blossoms in a spell to increase the abundance coming into your life?

Because it can only be worked during a particular season, drawing on the rhythms of the natural world, this is particularly potent magic. If you can time this spell with a waxing or Full Moon, you'll get a bonus boost of harmonious energy, but anytime during the Spring is fine.

Blossoms of apple, hawthorn, and honeysuckle are ideal if you can find them, but obviously use what blooms in your area. It's best to gather from the ground under and around the trees, but you can clip a bud or two directly from the branches if need be—just be sure to give thanks to tree as you do so. (You may want to leave an offering of a few drops of milk or honey.)

≣ YOU WILL NEED ≣

¼ to ½ cup blossom petals

White, pink, or green candle

+ Gather your blossoms the day before you plan to work the spell. Leave them to dry and charge overnight under moonlight.

+ Then, arrange the blossoms in a ring around the candle.

+ Spend a few moments meditating on the delights of Spring— the scents of flowers and warm soil, the buzzing of bees and the lengthening hours of daylight.

+ When you feel centered and in tune with the season, take a deep breath and light the candle as you say the following (or similar) words:

> *"Praises for the beauty of Spring,*
> *the miracles of new life all around.*
>
> *Let joy and growth in my life sing*
> *and endless abundance be found."*

+ Leave the candle to burn out on its own, if at all possible. Within 3 days, return the blossoms to the Earth by scattering them outside.

AUTUMN LEAVES
SPELL

Fans of natural magic will love working with the bright hues of red, orange, and yellow leaves at the peak of Autumn. This spell celebrates the most potent energies of the season—the explosion of color serving as a "grand finale" to the show that the trees have been putting on since the beginning of Spring.

Like the Spring Blossoms Spell (see pages 53–54) the seasonal aspect of this spell gives it its power—you are working with the magical rhythms of the natural world.

This time, the focus is on bringing forth the abundance you have been manifesting throughout the growing season, calling into your life whatever blessings and happy surprises have been ripening behind the scenes over the past months.

As with most abundance spells, if you work this during a waxing or Full Moon, you'll get a bonus boost of harmonious energy, but anytime during the Autumn is fine.

One crucial detail for this spell is that the leaves must be gathered from the ground. Just as you wouldn't harvest vegetables from your garden prematurely, don't pull leaves from the trees before they're ready to fall on their own.

Select the freshest, brightest, most blemish-free leaves you can find, and try to get a few different colors for maximum effect. (And if you live in an area where oak trees grow, be sure to select at least one leaf from this sacred tree!)

For a truly stunning display, press the leaves between two large, heavy books overnight so they will lay flat on your altar or work surface.

7 pressed leaves
Orange, brown, or yellow candle

═ INSTRUCTIONS ═

+ Arrange the leaves in a circle with the stems pointed inward, and place the candle in the center.

+ Spend a few moments meditating on the delights of Autumn— the cool, crisp air, the smell of smoldering bonfires, the crunching of leaves underfoot, and the lengthening of cozy evenings.

+ When you feel centered and in tune with the season, take a deep breath and light the candle as you say the following (or similar) words:

"As the sun's warmth wanes
and the nights grow longer,
the energies of Autumn
I gather and focus here.
As my very own wisdom and skills
grow stronger
Let the gifts of this season
in my life become clear."

+ Leave the candle to burn out on its own, if at all possible. If you like, let the leaves continue to decorate your space for a few days, until they fade and curl, and then scatter them back to the Earth.

PART THREE

HEALTH & WELL-BEING SPELLS

INTRODUCTION TO
HEALTH & WELL-BEING
SPELLS

IN OUR FAST-PACED AND OFTEN CHAOTIC WORLD, IT CAN BE difficult to maintain a healthy and positive state of well-being. Yet it's relatively easy to balance your own personal energy in order to face the challenges of this modern existence with motivation and endurance.

The spells in this section provide a range of approaches to decreasing the effects of stress and increasing your access to the reservoir of positive energy available to you in your daily life. However, while some of these spells can certainly be used to address physical health challenges, none are meant to replace any needed medical treatment. Be sure to always consult a health care professional for any serious concerns!

Of course, "well-being" is a very broad category that refers to more than just physical and emotional health. The energy of your environment is also crucial to your overall quality of life. Living with as little negative energy as possible is ideal, and to that end you'll find a few protection spells to enhance your physical and social environments and keep out unwanted energy.

As you try these spells, take note of their results, and use these experiences to help you expand and refine your own magical approach to your well-being.

SPEEDY RECOVERY
HEALING BATH

Anyone knows that a hot bath or shower all on its own can relieve a host of symptoms, from constriction in the chest to aches and pains to intestinal discomfort. And it's more and more widely known that adding some essential oils to the water can greatly enhance the healing effects.

But what happens when you also incorporate *magical intention* into your efforts? The next time you're feeling under the weather, try this spell and prepare to be amazed at the results!

As stated in the section introduction, this spell is not meant to replace any needed medical care, so if you're really ill, by all means consult your health care professional! But if you're dealing with a cold, flu, or other minor ailment that you wouldn't normally seek medical attention for, this healing bath is an excellent alternative to over-the-counter "medicines" that actually mask, rather than heal, the underlying source of your discomfort.

The physical properties of rosemary, juniper, and sandalwood—all ingredients in the Supportive Healing Oil blend (see page 106)—combine to fight infection and inflammation, as well as providing pain relief. The magical properties of these oils also, of course, include healing, as well as protection and longevity.

If you're unable to make your own batch of the Supportive Healing blend, look for commercially available blends that contain these three essential oils. (You may also be able to find them in a mineral bath blend. If you go this route, skip the sea salt.)

**5–7 drops Supportive Healing Oil
(see page 106)**

2–3 tablespoons sea salt

1 white candle

**Extra candles for atmosphere
(optional)**

≡ INSTRUCTIONS ≡

+ If using extra candles, light them first.

+ Run the bath until the tub is a quarter of the way full, and add the salt. As you sprinkle it over the water, say the following (or similar) words:

> *"The salt of the Earth removes
> this unwanted energy from my body."*

+ When the tub is halfway full, add the oil, saying the following, (or similar) words:

> *"The healing properties of these sacred oils
> restore me to my rightful state of balance."*

+ Now, as you light the white candle, say:

> *"So let it be."*

+ Turn off any artificial lighting in the bathroom, and climb into the tub. Stay in the bath for at least 20 minutes, breathing deeply with your eyes closed.

+ Focus on the scents of the healing oils and the feeling of the water on your skin. If your mind drifts to any subjects that make you feel anxious, simply release the thought and come back to noticing the positive sensations of the bath.

+ If you can, remain in the tub while draining the water, to enhance the purification vibration of the ritual.

+ After your bath, continue to take good care of yourself—be sure to drink plenty of fluids and get as much rest as you can. Know that you've just sped up your recovery time through magical action!

RITUAL TO
UNPLUG AND REALIGN

These days, most of us find ourselves at least somewhat addicted to our phones and other devices. When we spend too much time online, we can lose track of our connection to the physical world around us, and to our true selves.

Taking regular breaks from technology is good for physical, emotional, and spiritual health. This simple ritual helps you clear your energy field of excess electromagnetic field (EMF) radiation, and realign with the energies of Nature.

Shungite is a powerful absorber of EMF radiation, which can really affect energetically sensitive people. Orgonite and black tourmaline also work well. The alignment stone can be anything you resonate with personally, but those listed below are particularly effective.

=== YOU WILL NEED ===

1 absorption stone:
shungite, orgonite, or black tourmaline

1 alignment stone:
agate, amethyst, calcite, clear quartz,
lapis lazuli, or rose quartz

Journal or writing paper
(optional)

+ Before you begin, power down all electronics for at least two hours. Go for a walk if you like, or find a project to work on.

+ If you find this difficult, just notice how you react, without judging it. Are you antsy? Feeling isolated? Just sit with it and let it pass. How do you feel after 30 minutes? After two hours? If it helps, do some freewriting about your experience.

+ Find a place outdoors where you can sit with your bare feet on the Earth. (If this isn't possible, try taking a soak in the tub or a hot shower instead.)

+ Hold the absorption stone in both hands and visualize all excess electrical energy leaving your energy field and going into the stone. Take a few deep, meditative breaths. When you feel you've completely "unplugged" from the world of technology, set the stone down.

+ Now hold the alignment stone and visualize its energy connecting you to the Earth and to your inner self. Watch your breath as you hold this vision for a few moments. You may wish to journal about any insights, sensations, or intuitive messages that arise.

+ Repeat this ritual whenever you feel "zoned out" or disconnected from too much screen time.

ANXIETY CALMING SPELL

From time to time, everyone encounters a period of nonspecific anxiety that they just can't quite shake through positive thinking alone.

The aromatherapeutic properties of lavender and the calming effects of chamomile tea are useful anxiety combatants on their own, but the use of sage and stone give this spell extra power to really clear the anxious energy from your system.

Black crystals like jet, tourmaline, and obsidian are particularly useful for drawing away unwanted energy, but use any stone that calms you when you hold onto it, even if it's just an "ordinary" stone you find out in nature.

YOU WILL NEED

**Sage for smudging
(bundle or loose leaf)**

**Lavender incense,
or essential oil in a diffuser**

Chamomile tea

1 calming/grounding stone

+ Light the incense or heat the oil in the diffuser, then brew the tea. As the tea steeps, give yourself a gentle smudge with the sage to clear your energy field of unwanted energy (be sure to leave a window open—at least a crack—so the energy has somewhere to go).

+ Next, drink the tea while holding onto the stone. Visualize all anxious energy from within your body being pulled through your hands and into the stone.

+ When you feel ready, bury the stone outside. The Earth will neutralize the unwanted energy and it will not return to you.

RED JASPER
FOR ENERGY AND ENDURANCE

Although spells can be very powerful (and ideally fun), not all magic is enacted through formal spellwork. Crystals and other mineral stones are great examples of already-existing magic that simply needs to be harnessed in the right way in order to produce results.

Carrying stones on your person for extended periods of time is a great way to test out their effects on certain aspects of your life. Whether you're new to working with crystals, or just wanting to incorporate a new type of stone into your practice, the simple act of carrying a single stone for seven days can teach you more about that stone than any book could.

This example uses red jasper for the express purpose of enhancing energy and endurance, especially around dealing with unpleasant tasks.

YOU WILL NEED

1 medium-sized polished red jasper

Journal or other writing paper

INSTRUCTIONS

+ As with any stone, clear and charge your jasper before using it in magic.

+ Starting on a designated day, keep the stone with you in your pocket for seven days. Be sure to take it out and hold it in your hand several times a day.

+ At the end of each day—or at least at the end of the seven days—jot down any physical, emotional, or psychic impressions you've noticed, however subtle they may be.

+ As a next step, you may want to try this experiment again with a different stone and compare the results!

YELLOW INFUSION
"PICK ME UP"
SPELL

As you no doubt know, color has a powerful effect on our psychological state, and can be tremendously powerful in magic as well. This spell is focused on the color yellow and its abilities to raise our energetic vibration to a more cheerful frequency.

Yellow is the color most associated with sunlight, and can be enormously effective in boosting feelings of well-being and chasing away doubt, anxiety, and melancholy feelings. It's a great color to work with any time of year, but it can be particularly helpful in alleviating the winter doldrums!

You may or may not be able to acquire every ingredient listed below, but try to at least have one candle and two to three other yellow items, whether they are crystals, flowers, or even ribbons or pieces of fabric. This is literally a case of "the more, the merrier," but don't refrain from working the spell simply because you don't have everything on the list.

Regarding the music—while everyone's taste is different, be sure to choose something that makes you feel positive, upbeat emotion. You may absolutely *love* music that's full of angst and sadness, and that's fine, but it's not the right vibrational frequency for this type of spellwork, so find something happy to listen to!

For maximum effects, try wearing something yellow while working the spell, whether it's clothing or hair accessories—even a raincoat can do the trick!

1 or more yellow candles
(reserve 1 as the spell candle)

A vase with yellow flowers,
such as daffodils, sunflowers,
or dandelions

1 or more yellow crystals, such
as citrine, topaz, amber,
yellow fluorite, or tiger's eye

A recording of upbeat,
cheerful music

A yellow cloth covering
for your altar or work space
(optional)

Cheerful images with
predominantly yellow
coloring, such as a Sun card
from a Tarot deck (optional)

≡ INSTRUCTIONS ≡

+ First, put on the music.

+ Then arrange your altar or other work space in a way that's
pleasing to your eye. Cover it with yellow cloth, if using, and then
place the crystals, flowers, candles, and any other imagery you're
incorporating into the spell. If you have more candles than just the
spell candle, light them now.

+ Then, hold one or more crystals between your palms, and spend a
few moments envisioning yourself in a very happy scene, whether
it's a party attended by all of your favorite people, a walk in nature,
a trip to the tropics—whatever daydream lights you up the most.
Hang out in this "fantasyland" for as long as you like.

+ When you feel noticeably better than you did at the start of the
spell, light the spell candle.

+ Allow it to burn all the way down, knowing as it does that
you will feel a significant lift in your mood for at least two to
three days.

+ If you can, leave your altar/work space decked out in yellow
for awhile, and gaze at all that yellow as frequently as you can.
Repeat this spell as often as you like.

ENERGY CLEANSING
BODY SCRUB

This body scrub is not intended to clean physical dirt, but rather nonphysical energetic debris, which all of us accumulate in our energy field in the course of our daily interactions in the world. Coconut oil has amazing healing and purifying properties, while Himalayan salt helps to remove energetic attachments.

Add one or more of your favorite essential oils to this dynamic duo for an even more enhanced lifting and clearing effect. Good choices include bergamot, cedarwood, clary sage, geranium, lavender, patchouli, peppermint (be sparing), rosemary, sandalwood, and vetiver. Keep in mind that some oils, such as clove, can irritate the skin, so do some research into any oil you're not sure about.

You can also tailor the recipe to a magical purpose in addition to the energetic clearing, if you wish. For example, include patchouli and bergamot for prosperity, lavender and clary sage for healing, or geranium for a cheerful start to your day.

½ cup coconut oil

1 cup fine grain Himalayan salt

small mason jar or other container

mortar & pestle
(optional)

10–30 drops* essential oil(s)

═ INSTRUCTIONS ═

+ Place the coconut oil in the jar. If the oil is solid, melt it to liquid by placing the jar in a bowl of very warm (not boiling) water for a few minutes.

+ Grind the salt into a fine powder with the mortar and pestle, if needed.

+ In batches, add the salt to the jar and mix with oil thoroughly until you get a good scrub-like consistency. (You may need to add a bit more salt or a bit more oil, depending on the size of the salt grains.)

+ Add essential oils of your choice, stirring and testing the scent of the scrub as you go. If you're adding a specific magical intention, visualize your desired outcome while you work.

+ Try using this scrub in the shower every day for a week, and take note of how much better you feel as unwanted negative energy is cleared out of your system!

---

* If the coconut oil is quite fragrant, you will need more drops of the essential oils to bring out their scents.

NOTE: Coconut oil can make for a slippery tub or shower floor, so use caution and clean up thoroughly after each use of the scrub.

"BUSY BEE"
BALANCING TALISMAN

While some people truly thrive on being so busy they don't have time to think, most magical types, with their higher levels of sensitivity and creativity, don't tend to enjoy these situations at all!

If you've got a busy day or week coming up and feel yourself dreading it, here's a relaxing spell to help you get through this time with greater ease and comfort. You may even want to make this a regular ritual, perhaps at the beginning of your workweek!

If you don't have any crystals or other mineral stones, use any small "worry" stone that you can carry in your pocket.

≡ YOU WILL NEED ≡

**1 cup of chamomile tea
(ideally sweetened with honey)**

1 white candle

**1 piece of jade, rose quartz,
amethyst, or other
calming stone**

**Lavender or
other calming incense
(optional)**

+ Light the incense, if using, and brew the tea. As the tea steeps, light the candle and gaze at the flame for a few moments.

+ Take a few sips of the tea and a few deep breaths. Then place the stone in your dominant palm and place your other palm on top, cradling the stone and charging it with calming, peaceful energy.

+ Say the following (or similar) words:

> *"I have infinite time,*
> *in my sacred space, with peace*
> *and calm to go at my pace.*
>
> *I bring this calm to the day(s) ahead,*
> *peacefully moving wherever*
> *I'm led."*

+ Pass the stone briefly above the candle flame three times.

+ It is now charged to assist you in your busy times—just carry it in your pocket and hold it whenever you feel the need.

MAGIC MOTIVATION MORNING POTION

This very simple potion is really an enhanced version of the morning ritual that most people already engage in, though perhaps not very consciously—the all-important cup of coffee! However, non-caffeine drinkers can also make a pleasant morning brew for themselves, ideally with an herbal tea that goes well with cinnamon.

Use this potion as an extra, magical boost for days when you feel lagging but have a lot to do.*

The visualization and reciting of the spell is ideally done out-doors, but facing a window is also perfectly fine.

---

* If you're lagging due to illness or being run-down, it's best to stick to an herbal version, rather than ingesting caffeine.

1 fresh brewed cup of coffee or tea

1 pinch of cinnamon

1 teaspoon or more honey

≡ INSTRUCTIONS ≡

+ Stir the honey, if using, into your beverage, using clockwise motions. (If not using honey, stir it clockwise anyway.)

+ While the liquid is still turning circles, sprinkle the cinnamon into the center.

+ Take your potion outside or to a window, and thank the morning light (no matter how cloudy the day may actually be) for showing you the way into your day.

+ Take a relaxing breath and begin sipping your beverage.

+ Visualize feeling energy and clarity as you forge ahead with your day, and the satisfaction of meeting your goals.

+ When you're ready, say the following (or similar) words:

"I greet this day in gratitude.
I sail through this day on my positive attitude.

As my energy now rises, I know I will meet
all of my tasks until they're complete.

So let it be."

+ Now get moving, and enjoy your day!

HOMEWORK MARATHON
ENDURANCE SPELL

For those grueling final weeks of a college semester, or for simply catching up on school work when you're behind, try this spell for bolstering your confidence and focus. (You don't have to be a student to benefit from this spell, however—you can also use it for finishing up a project for a job if you like!)

Fresh flower petals are ideal, if you can find them, but dried will work just as well in a pinch.

YOU WILL NEED

1 orange or yellow candle

1 teaspoon orchid, honeysuckle, lilac,
or hibiscus petals

1 piece of quartz crystal or amethyst

Lemon or rosemary oil

+ Sprinkle the flower petals on a plate or on your altar/work surface. Anoint the candle with the oil, and then roll it in the petals.

+ Set the candle in its holder and place the quartz or amethyst next to it.

+ Visualize yourself being finished with the homework or project you're working on. Allow yourself to feel the relief and elation that you know you'll experience when this work is done.

+ When you're ready, light the candle as you say the following (or similar) words:

"For the energy, and focus
to complete my task
Your continued assistance,
spirit, I ask."

+ Place the crystal on your desk (or other work surface) for the duration of your "marathon."

+ Whenever you feel discouraged or unfocused, hold the stone in your hands for a few moments.

SPELL TO BIND
A TROUBLEMAKER

Positive and ethically sound magic focuses on respecting the free will of others, and does not seek to actively manipulate the behavior or circumstances of anyone other than the caster of the spell.

However, this doesn't mean that magical means can't be used to shield you from the ill intentions of others. This can include passive-aggressive coworkers who try to sabotage your success, or exes who keep trying to engage you in drama long after you've broken up.

Of course, it's best to try to work out conflicts through honest dialogue, but if this isn't possible, a little magical intervention can do the trick.

The use of string and knot-work is a long-standing tradition in magic. The energy of your intention is concentrated into the knot, and either sealed, or later released, depending on the spell.

In binding work, the knot "traps" any negative energy the person may have in relation to you. Burying the string in the Earth then neutralizes the energy, allowing you to begin healing from whatever negativity you encountered through your interactions with this person*.

Any type of string, cord, or ribbon will do as long as you can tie tight knots in it. If it's too thick or slippery to hold a knot, the spell will not be as effective.

---

* Do not envision any harm coming to this person, even if it feels to you like "karmic justice" would be served. Simply focus on banishing their ability to do you any harm—physical, psychic, or otherwise.

1 black or white work candle

1 piece of string, 8–12 inches (20.3–30.5 cm) in length

━━ INSTRUCTIONS ━━

- Light the candle, and lay the string out flat in front of you.

- Spend a few moments envisioning yourself surrounded by white light. Do not dwell on your issues with this person, but rather focus on feeling centered and at peace.*

- When you're ready, tie a knot in the string, a third of the way in from the left, while saying:

  *"I bind any and all negativity aimed at me
  from [name of person]."*

- Then tie a second knot two thirds of the way in, saying:

  *"I bind any further conflict between me
  and this person."*

- Finally, tie the third knot, which should be roughly a third of the way in from the right, and say:

  *"I seal this working with my highest personal
  power, for the greatest good."*

- As you bury the string, visualize it disintegrating into the soil. If you can't bury it in the Earth, use a bowl of salt instead, and then discard the salt in an outdoor trash receptacle.

PROTECTION SPELL
FOR PETS

While we are, generally speaking, bound to outlive most of our animal companions, we can draw on magical resources to keep them safe and healthy throughout their natural lives. This all-around protection blessing is tailored for cats and dogs, but can be used on other pets as well.*

YOU WILL NEED

Sea salt

INSTRUCTIONS

+ Mark a sacred circle with the sea salt, sit in the center, and call your pet to you.

✦ With your hands on your pet's head (or body, if need be) say the following (or similar) words:

"Guardian spirits**, I hereby ask
keep (name of pet) within your grasp throughout
each night and each passing day.

Let (name of pet) not be tempted to stray
beyond the boundaries of safety
or the joys of good health,
let our happy companionship
provide emotional wealth.

With this blessing, (name of pet)
is safe and sound,
(his/her) marvelous being,
protection will surround.

So let it be."

✦ Afterward, sweep up the salt, and be sure to spend some special time cuddling with your pet to seal the blessing.

---

* Your pet may be curious about the salt circle and want to lick it. While large quantities of salt are not healthy for pets (or people), using a thin line of salt for the circle should not pose a problem. Just use your best judgment— if salt on the floor is going to be too much of a distraction to keep your pet in the circle, try using small crystals or pebbles instead.

** If you work with a particular deity, especially if that deity is known to be associated with animal magic, feel free to address deity by name, either in lieu of or in addition to "guardian spirits."

WITCH BOTTLE
FOR PROTECTING
THE HOME

Witch bottles represent a magical tradition that goes back centuries. Also known as "spell bottles," they were mostly used to repel negative energies, often from a specific source, such as a feared adversary. Traditionally, they contained some rather unsavory ingredients—like hair and blood—and were buried in the ground to work their magic.

Modern witch bottles are employed for a variety of purposes, including love and wealth, and generally don't involve human ingredients (although some traditionalists still use the old recipes). They may still be buried, but are also hidden in the home and even displayed openly in some cases, depending on the purpose of the bottle and the preferences of its creator.

This particular protective spell calls for hiding the bottle, but you can leave it visible if that appeals to you more. (It's not at all necessary to bury it, but if you feel strongly called to do so, for whatever reason, then go for it.)

You can also personalize the spell in other ways, as you'll see below, by choosing the ingredients that make the most sense to you. Just be sure to include at least something from each category—herbs, crystals, and sharp metal objects.

The items in this last group act as an energetic "fence" by mimicking a physical barbed wire fence, warding off negative or harmful energies or intentions. Obviously, take care when handling these—feel free to wear gloves!

Once you get the hang of it, you can make a witch bottle for any purpose, provided you work with ingredients appropriate to the purpose. Be creative and work with what inspires you most.

═ YOU WILL NEED ═

- 1 empty glass bottle with a cork (wine or olive bottles work well, but you can also cork a soda or beer bottle)

- ¼ cup soil (for best results, dig soil from your yard) or sea salt

- 1 (minimum) protective crystal: obsidian, onyx, black tourmaline, or smoky quartz

- 3 cloves of garlic, crushed

  A pinch of rose thorns or stinging nettles

- 3 bay leaves

- 3 (minimum) nails, sewing needles, and/or other sharp metal objects

- 1 tablespoon (minimum) of 1 or more protective herbs: basil, dill, fennel, juniper, rosemary, tarragon

  Vinegar (any kind will do, but apple cider is a popular choice)

- 1 black candle

  Dried sage—loose leaf or smudge stick (optional)

+ If you have sage on hand, it's nice to smudge your altar or work space before constructing the bottle, but it's not strictly necessary. Some people also like to charge the empty bottle in moonlight the night before, but this is also optional.

+ Once you're ready to begin, light the black candle and say the following (or similar) words:

> *"Protective spirits, attend my work*
> *and add your power to mine.*
>
> *As I create this magic for my home,*
> *grant me your protection divine."*

+ Now, add the soil or salt, making sure it covers the bottom of the bottle. Next, add the crystal, the crushed garlic, and the nettles or thorns.

+ Give the bottle a gentle shake at this point, and then add the bay leaves, the sharp metal objects, and the rest of the herbs.

+ Pour the vinegar in until the bottle is full, but be sure to leave enough room for the cork to go in. Cork the bottle and give it another shake as you say the following (or similar) words:

> *"Protective spirits, honor my work*
> *and add your power to mine.*
>
> *Now the power within this bottle*
> *grants my home protection divine.*
>
> *It is done."*

- Now seal the work by holding the candle wick over the top of the bottle until a few drops of melted wax have landed on the cork.

- Hide the bottle somewhere near the entrance of your home.

PART FOUR

ASSORTED
SPELLS &
STRATEGIES

INTRODUCTION TO
ASSORTED SPELLS &
STRATEGIES

THERE ARE SO MANY DIFFERENT STYLES, TECHNIQUES, and forms of magic —many of which are just being discovered in our time—that the possibilities are endless. This section serves as a brief introduction to various approaches to magic, including kitchen witchery, making your own ingredients, and using timing and the rhythms of the natural world to your advantage.

Although a few of these spells have fairly specific aims, many of them can be considered "all-purpose" and therefore can still be applied to the areas of love and relationships, wealth and prosperity, and/or health and well-being. But if you have a desire or concern that doesn't fit neatly into one of those categories—and we all do, at one point or another—try using one or more of the spells below to address it.

In these pages you'll find spells focused around tools sourced directly from nature, new ways to request information from the Universe, recipes for creating your own oil blends, and a set of magical workings based on the cycles of the Moon. Finally, you'll discover a ritual for celebrating your own personal new year and setting yourself up for 12 months of magical manifestation!

Enjoy yourself as you experiment with these spells, keep track of your results, and continue exploring further the wide world of magic.

GOOD NEWS
SPELL

This is a good spell for beginners, or for anyone wanting a little practice in focusing on an intention with rather low stakes, but fun results.

You'll be delightfully surprised by the ways this spell can come back to you. The trick is to be general in your request—don't ask for good news regarding matters you're overly anxious about at the moment, or any kind of specific outcome, since this can really muddy the energy you're sending out.

Once you've worked the spell, release it and forget about it—you can, of course, keep an ear out for good news, but trust that it will arrive for you without your having to be "on the alert."

Because of the relatively short time frame for the spell, it's ideal to use a spell candle or other short-burning candle, and let it burn all the way out. Whichever color you choose, go for as bright a hue as possible, as a high vibrational frequency is key for this kind of working.

1 yellow, gold, orange,
or green candle

Essential oil of bergamot,
cinnamon, or patchouli

INSTRUCTIONS

- Anoint the candle with a drop or two of the oil.

- Focus on the feeling of receiving some happy news from out of the blue—if it helps, call up a memory of such a time in your past.

- When you have a lock on the feeling, repeat the following words three times:

    "Within three days arrives
    a happy surprise to brighten my day
    in a wonderful way."

- Light the candle and seal the spell by saying

    "So let it be."

CLEANSING
RAIN WALK

For many people, a rainy day is a reason to stay indoors, or else shelter under an umbrella if they have to go outside. But did you know that rain is one of nature's most magical ingredients? It's particularly good for cleansing the aura of stale or negative energy, especially when you're dealing with a persistent emotional challenge.

This spell makes use of rain's healing vibrations, and requires no ingredients other than yourself, your intention, some focused words, and of course, some rain!

A short walk in the rain is ideal, but if this isn't possible, simply standing outside will also work. The invocation below works well and can be repeated as many times as you like while you're in the rain.

You can also tailor it to fit any particular challenge you may be dealing with at the moment. Simply substitute your issue for "all that I no longer need."

A rainy day!

+ When it starts to rain, head outside for a short walk (or simply stand outside).

+ Focus and say the following words of intention (or invent your own):

> *"Spirit of rain, loving water,*
> *release all that I no longer need and renew me*
> *for the blessed times ahead."*

+ How long you stay out in the rain is up to you, but a general rule of thumb is at least five minutes. If it's a very light rain, you'll want to take longer, but if it's a downpour, just a few minutes will probably do the trick.

+ Of course, be sure *not* to work this spell in a lightning storm!

THREE WISHES
BIRTHDAY
SPELL

Making a wish before blowing out the candles on a cake is a time-honored custom at birthday celebrations. Typically, the tradition calls for the wish to be kept secret. This is perhaps due to a subconscious understanding that any doubtful thoughts arising from speaking it out loud can thwart the manifestation of the wish.

This spell is meant to be worked in solitude, where you can speak your wishes aloud to the Universe with no one else to hear you. It's also an opportunity to reflect upon and celebrate your life experiences over the past year, before setting intentions for what you'd like to manifest in the year to come.

Dandelions are also associated with wishes, as seen in the tradition of making a wish before blowing the seeds from the "puff ball" (or seed head) of a mature flower. If you have a birthday during dandelion season, try working with a live seed-head. If not, dried dandelion leaf will work just as well.

Don't worry if you're unable to work this spell on your actual birthday. Any time within the week before or after that date will still be energetically favorable for this work.

Your birthday candle can be any color. Go with your personal favorite color, a color corresponding to one or more of your wishes, or any color you're drawn to work with.

1 work candle for atmosphere

1 "birthday" spell candle

Journal or writing paper

Parchment paper
(optional)

3-inch (1 cm) length of ribbon

Pinch of dried dandelion leaf
(or live seed head)

≡ INSTRUCTIONS ≡

+ Light the work candle, and then take some time to journal about what has unfolded for you over the past 12 months.

+ Take care to focus only on what you appreciate—highlights, accomplishments, funny moments, and the like. What did you learn about yourself over the course of the year? How have you progressed spiritually, and/or in your magical practice?

+ Honor yourself for any difficulties you've made it through, but don't dwell on them. They are in the past.

+ Now, identify three manifestations you'd like to bring forth over the coming year. Take some time to journal about them in detail, if you like. Then write a word or short phrase representing each wish on a small piece of parchment or writing paper.

- ✦ Lay the paper on your altar and light the spell candle.

- ✦ Place the pinch of dandelion leaf in the palm of your hand. (If using a live flower, hold it by the stem.) Speak your three wishes aloud, and then say the following (or similar) words:

"Birthday wishes, numbered three,
now become reality.

One more year around the Sun,
by this date next it will be done."

- ✦ Gently blow the dandelion leaf/seeds so they scatter over the paper.

- ✦ Roll the paper up into a scroll and tie the ribbon around it.

- ✦ Set it in front of the birthday candle until the candle burns out on its own.

- ✦ Keep this record of your wishes on your altar for as long as you like, then store it somewhere special until your next birthday.

BURNING QUESTION
CLARITY SPELL

When you're faced with a tough dilemma or a difficult decision, it can be hard not to obsess about it, even if you know that doing so doesn't help you arrive at an answer. This spell is good for opening up any blocked channels that you may have around the question that are preventing an answer from coming through.

This is not ideal for yes-or-no answers to an outcome you have no direct control over, such as whether or not you'll get that job you applied for. The goal here is clarity about a situation that requires action on your part. If you don't have a cauldron or other fireproof dish, you can place the burning paper in a sink.

═══ YOU WILL NEED ═══

1 black, gold, violet, indigo, or white candle

Small strip (3–5 inches [7.6–12.7 cm])
of parchment or other paper

Small cauldron or heat-resistant dish

═══ INSTRUCTIONS ═══

+ Light the candle.

+ Ground and center yourself, and hold your question for a moment in your mind, *without* allowing yourself to mentally rehash any of the details surrounding it.

+ When you have a clear sense of how to phrase your question as briefly and directly as possible, write it on the strip of paper.

- As you ignite the paper, say

  *"I release my question to the benevolent spirit
  and open my ears to the answer."*

- Hold the strip as it burns for as long as is safe, and then drop it in the cauldron or sink.

- Now trust that the answer will come to you when the time is right, and put your mind on something pleasant and relaxing.

CHICORY VICTORY CHARM

For getting past any resistance to a goal you've been struggling with—losing weight, finding a new job, quitting an unhealthy habit, and so on—try working with chicory root.

Chicory is used for eliminating obstacles of all kinds, and its traditional uses included removing curses and opening locks for which no key was available. It was said in ancient times to confer invisibility, which was not likely a literal belief, but a way of describing the effects of becoming invulnerable to negative energy of any kind.

Carrying the root in the form of this simple charm can help you overcome your current obstacles.

Chicory root is usually available in a few different forms. For this spell, avoid the powdered root, and go with raw cut root or granules instead.

YOU WILL NEED

1 tablespoon chicory root

Cauldron or bowl

Small (4 × 4 inch [10 × 10 cm])
square of cloth

INSTRUCTIONS

+ Place the chicory in your cauldron or bowl, and mix it around with your fingers, to infuse the root with your own personal energy (be sure to wash your hands before beginning this spell).

+ As you do this, say the following (or similar) words:

"I am invisible to the energy of obstruction.
I easily find the path of least resistance to achieve my goal.
With this working, it is done."

+ Lay the cloth out flat and place the chicory into the center.

+ Tie the corners together to create a secure bundle.

+ Carry it in your pocket or purse, or wear it on a cord around your neck.

+ When you've achieved your goal, thank the powers that be and either bury your bundle or untie it and scatter the chicory on the Earth.

EGG MAGIC
FOR NEW BEGINNINGS

Eggs have held mystical and magical significance around the world since ancient times, and are still used in many magical traditions today. Egg shells are crushed and powdered for protection workings, while raw eggs are powerful agents in healing spells. Eggs also symbolize fertility, springtime, abundance, and pure potential.

In this spell, you will charge and then bury a raw egg with the intention for something new you wish to bring into your life experience. The egg is a perfect symbol of a new beginning, as it literally houses the physical substances that manifest new life. This makes it an ideal technique for those wishing to bring a child into the world, but it can also be used to start a new business, bring in a new career opportunity, or support a new self-care endeavor, such as a diet or exercise program.

You will also harness the energies of the Sun and the cardinal direction of East to add powerful strength to the work. For best results, work this spell on a night during the first half of the waxing phase of the Moon, and bury the egg first thing the following morning.

1 green, brown, or white
pillar candle

1 raw egg

Olive oil

Bowl of soil (or sand, straw,
or hay), with enough to cover
the top of the egg

+ Light the candle and anoint the egg with a drop or two
  of the oil.

+ Hold the egg gently in your clasped hands and visualize it filling
  with a bright, pure, pale orange light that radiates through the
  shell to surround your body. See yourself thoroughly enjoying
  the results of what you are now just setting into motion.

+ Spend a few moments here, strengthening your vision. Then,
  when you feel ready, simply say "*And so it is.*"

+ Place the egg in the bowl and gently cover it with the soil
  or straw.

+ Leave it on your altar overnight, and then bury it at sunrise in
  the easternmost portion of your yard.

+ The candle can be extinguished before you go to bed, and
  re-lit whenever you like, to remind yourself of the magical new
  beginnings taking place in the soil of your life.

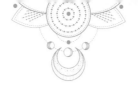

AVOCADO BEAUTY
SPELL

This spell is a great example of kitchen witchery, as it makes use of both the physical and magical properties of one of nature's spectacular edible gifts—the delicious avocado!

Treasured since ancient times for both its calming and aphrodisiac effects, avocado has been used to promote love, beauty, and relaxation in many magical traditions. Some Witches favor the wood of the branches for use in fertility magic. Many follow the practice of carrying an avocado pit to promote love and beauty.

This fruit has also made a comeback in modern beauty products, since its high content of healthy fats and minerals makes it an excellent moisturizer and soothing on the skin.

In this delicious spell, the avocado works on both the physical and invisible planes to refresh and restore your body, which always has the effect of making us appear more beautiful to others.

The main magical act is to eat the avocado with a spoon, straight out of the skin (if you like, try adding just a pinch of salt to bring out the flavor even more!) but the energy of the spell is enhanced with a magic circle made from dried flower petals.

Be sure you have enough petals to mark a wide enough circle to sit within. Some people like to use fresh flowers in several vases instead, which is also great, if you have an abundance of flowers. You can also get creative and use a combination of the two.

It's ideal to work this spell outdoors in the sunlight, but if this isn't possible, sit indoors in a room with direct sunlight coming in. If you have to work the spell at night, light several candles and place them just outside the circle.

1 avocado

   Plate, knife and spoon

   Sea salt (optional)

Fresh flowers and/or flower petals

5–7 candles (if working at night)

≡ INSTRUCTIONS ≡

+ Starting in your kitchen, hold the avocado gently in your palms, close your eyes, and take a deep breath. Visualize a beautiful white light radiating from your skin.

+ Slice the avocado in half. Scoop out and rinse the pit, and set it on the plate. Sprinkle the salt (if using) across the two cut halves of the avocado. Set the plate where the center of your circle will be.

+ Now create your circle with the flower petals, silently thanking the powers of nature that have come together in order to provide you with such a beautiful setting to work your magic in.

+ Once you're settled inside the circle, eat your avocado. Take your time and really savor the flavor. When you're done, close your eyes and say the following (or similar) words:

> *"Nature, thank you for nourishing*
> *my beauty with your own."*

+ As for the avocado pit, you can compost it if you'd like, but first try wrapping it in a cloth and carrying it with you for a few days to strengthen your feeling of improved beauty.

+ If you live in a tropical or subtropical area, try planting the pit to grow your very own avocado tree!

MAGICAL OILS

If you've been exploring magic for a while, you've most likely come across spells that call for a blended magical oil of one kind or another, such as banishing oil for repelling negative energy.

There are some fine, high-quality oil blends available at Wiccan and other New Age shops, as well as through online vendors. However, it can be well worth purchasing a few single essential oils and creating your own magical blends. Then you can use the rest of the individual oils for healing, cleaning, and many other purposes.

Here are 3 magical blends to try, using oils that are highly valued for their diverse uses. You can get dropper bottles at most health food stores or online. Tiny screw-top jars can also work in a pinch.

≡ YOU WILL NEED ≡

- ¼ cup carrier oil (almond, olive, grape seed, jojoba or safflower oil)
- 1 small dropper bottle for each blend
- 1 vial of each essential oil in the recipe

SUPPORTIVE HEALING OIL
(used in *Speedy Recovery Healing Bath*, on pages 62–64):

- ✦ 4 drops rosemary
- ✦ 2 drops juniper
- ✦ 1 drop sandalwood

WEALTH ATTRACTION OIL
(used in *Calling in the Cash*, on pages 36–37):

- ✦ 3 drops bergamot
- ✦ 1 drop basil
- ✦ 1 drop patchouli
- ✦ 1 drop sandalwood

PEACE OF MIND OIL
(used in the Choosing Peace in Tough Situations, on pages 22–23):

- ✦ 3 drops ylang-ylang
- ✦ 3 drops lavender
- ✦ 2 drops chamomile
- ✦ 1 drop bergamot

MIXING

- ✦ Essential oils are volatile and highly concentrated, and most are too strong for direct contact with skin. A base oil, or carrier oil, creates a safe medium for the essential oils to blend together. Once blended with the carrier oil, they can be safely used for anointing candles and other magical tools, as well as on skin, if desired.

- ✦ To avoid problems be sure not to skip the carrier oil.

CHARGING

- ✦ It's ideal to visualize your intent while creating your magical oil blends.

- ✦ Playing elevating music while you work is very helpful in enhancing the energy of the finished product.

- ✦ Once you've put the cap on your new blend, be sure to hold the bottle between your palms and send your personal magical power into its contents.

USING

- ✦ Use your oil as directed in spellwork, to anoint candles and other magical tools, as a fragrance, and/or as a gift.

- ✦ Store in a cool dark place, and aim to use the whole bottle within one year's time.

ATMOSPHERIC
CRYSTAL GRIDDING

Crystal gridding is a simple and subtle way to keep your space clear of unwanted energy and promote a peaceful atmosphere. The process below can be used for a single room or your entire home.

Smoky quartz or another protective stone can be substituted for the tourmaline; just make sure all four stones are the same type. The center stone can really be any stone that resonates with you, but the three listed will serve well to promote positive energy. Choose according to your intuition.

≡ YOU WILL NEED ≡

**4 pieces black tourmaline
or smoky quartz**

4 small selenite wands

**1 medium-to-large "center stone"
(rose quartz, amethyst, or citrine)**

Sage wand for smudging

+ Before you begin, cleanse and charge all crystals for several hours in sunlight (ideally a full day).

+ Then give each room in your home a good cleaning, eliminating dust and clutter as much as possible.

+ Smudge each room with the sage, making sure to leave a window or door open for the energy to exit through.

+ Place one black tourmaline in each corner of the home.

+ Then place a selenite wand in front of each tourmaline so that one end points to the stone and the other to the center of the home.

+ Place the center stone on a table or shelf where it will be seen daily, as close to the physical center of the home as possible.

+ Sit here for a moment and activate the grid by visualizing all the stones connecting to each other energetically.

+ Then say the following (or similar) words:

"My home is safe, peaceful,
positive, and clear.
Blessed Be."

+ Cleanse and recharge your stones (especially the tourmaline) periodically.

+ If you start to feel negativity in your home, it's time to cleanse and reactivate the grid.

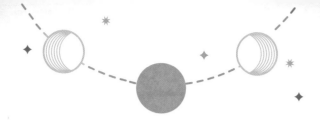

NEW MOON
INTENTION SETTING

Setting and following an intention for the entire waxing phase of the moon is a good way to deepen your relationship to the movement of the moon's cycle and strengthen your personal power.

The nightly ritual of adding a stone to the bowl, which represents the gradual but steady increase of the moon's appearance over a two-week span, keeps you connected to the energy of your manifestation as it takes shape.

The stones should fit in one layer at the bottom of the bowl for maximum visual effect. You will need a designated space to keep this magical working going for the duration of the waxing phase, whether it's an altar, a shelf, or even the center of your kitchen table.

This work is ideal for supporting a positive change you want to make in your life, such as starting a new exercise routine or breaking out of a rut.

Traditionally, the waxing moon is considered to be the time for calling something into your life, rather than shedding something from your life, but as always, you should do what your intuition tells you.

This should be begun on the evening closest to the actual time that the moon becomes new, but if this isn't possible, start at the closest possible time afterward.

1 small bowl, ideally ceramic or clay

A minimum of 15 small stones or pebbles, ideally round and similarly sized

1 white or silver pillar or votive candle

Journal or book of shadows (or other paper)

═ INSTRUCTIONS ═

+ Ground and center yourself, and light the candle with a greeting to the New Moon, using whatever words suit you.

+ Write for a few moments about your goal in your journal, or book of shadows if you use one for this type of work, to create a mental picture of how your life will look/feel when you've accomplished it.

+ If you wish, write a short sentence stating your goal, and keep it with the candle and bowl for the duration of the spell. Alternatively, you can use an image that represents your intention.

+ Now, just spend a few moments gazing at the candle flame, and visualize your intention manifesting with ease and joy. When you're ready, take the first stone in your dominant hand and say the following (or similar) words:

> *"As the night receives your light and*
> *the oceans feel your pull, I set my intention*
> *to grow with you, from New to Full."*

+ Place the stone in the bowl. Every night until the Full Moon, relight the candle and place another stone in the bowl.

+ Once the moon is full, review the progress you've made toward your goal, thank the moon for her assistance, and remove the stones.

HALF-MOON SPELLS

Much attention is given to the New Moon and Full Moon as potent times for magic—and for good reason! However, the midpoints between these two phases of the Moon's cycle can also be significant occasions, especially for taking stock of any progress in areas of your life that are important to you at this time.

These dates can also be useful when you're in the mood to practice some magic, but can't quite decide on a specific goal, or even a point in time.

Check your calendar for the next half-moon, and then find the corresponding magical associations for the day it falls on. Then you can start planning to work a spell for an appropriate purpose on that night!

You can also try the two spells below for some mid-cycle moon magic.

WAXING HALF-MOON SPELL
(First Quarter)

Also known as the First Quarter Moon, the Waxing Half-Moon marks the midpoint between the planting and the full ripening of our intentions. Whatever new manifestation you've been working toward is ideally starting to make itself apparent, even if just in the form of new ideas that can help you achieve your goals.

This spell directs the lunar energy into building on the energetic momentum you've achieved so far by using moonstones to create a "cairn" of sorts. Small pieces of moonstone are widely available at magic and other New Age shops, but if you can't find any, try gathering several smooth, round stones from a nearby beach or creek.

This spell can also be worked in conjunction with New Moon Intention Setting spell (see pages 110–11) as a sort of energetic "boost" halfway through the course of that spell.

But don't worry if you didn't set a specific intention at the most recent New Moon. You can work this spell in regard to any intention that you've ever set and are still interested in. The point is to mark your progress and renew your energetic dedication to further manifestation.

≡ YOU WILL NEED ≡

**Several pieces (3 minimum)
moonstone**

1 white or silver candle

**Journal, book of shadows, or other paper
(optional)**

+ Hold the stones in your hands for several moments, attuning to their energy.

+ Spend some time reflecting on your goal, and what has manifested in your life in relationship to that goal—no matter how small or insignificant it may seem to you at times.

+ It's very helpful to do some freewriting about this, especially if it's a goal you feel yourself to be struggling with. You need to be able to identify some measure of success—even if it's still only at the idea stage—in order for the spell to be effective.

+ Once you're focused positively on a sense of progress, light the candle. Then stack the stones on top of each other to form a cairn. It's okay if your cairn looks more like a pile of rocks than a completely vertical stack—the point is that you're representing the energy of building on your prior success. Feel free to play around with the stones until you get a cairn that you're satisfied with.

+ Then, using your own words, give thanks for what you have manifested so far, express your intention for continued growth and progress, and acknowledge the need to trust in the process of manifestation.

+ If you like, leave the cairn out where you'll see it from now until the Full Moon.

WANING HALF-MOON SPELL
(Third Quarter)

The waning Moon is traditionally the time for releasing and even banishing unwanted phenomena from your life, whether it be a habit of thought, an unhealthy relationship, an addiction, or a karmic pattern of some kind.

Technically, any time from the second night after the Full Moon until the eve of the New Moon is good for this type of magic, but the third-quarter mark is a nice halfway point.

One advantage of working for release or decrease on this night is that it gives you a week to experience the effects before it's time to set new intentions again at the New Moon.

Smoky quartz is a variety of quartz crystal strongly associated with the waning and dark phases of the Moon. In this spell, it works with the water—which is ruled by the Moon—to wash away the unwanted from your life. If you don't have smoky quartz, clear quartz crystal will also work, but it's worth the extra effort to acquire a piece or two of smoky quartz for its grounding and protective energies.

≡ YOU WILL NEED ≡

- 1 piece smoky quartz
- 1 Mason jar or other jar with screw-top lid
- Water
- 1 black or silver candle
- Journal, book of shadows, or other paper (optional)

✦ Spend a few minutes reflecting and (ideally) freewriting on what it is you want to release, decrease, or banish.

✦ Don't focus your attention on the issue itself, but instead visualize the relief and freedom you will feel when you've cleared it from your life.

✦ When you feel ready, light the candle.

✦ Hold the smoky quartz between your palms and visualize the energy of this unwanted phenomena being pulled from you and your energy field into the stone.

✦ Put the stone in the jar of water, close the lid, and give the jar a gentle shake.

✦ Leave it outside under the moon, or in the nearest windowsill, overnight. In the morning, pour the water out onto the Earth*.

✦ You can bury the stone, if that feels appropriate, or else cleanse it thoroughly and charge it under direct moonlight for several hours.

---

* It's best to discard the water outdoors, and directly onto soil. If this isn't possible, you can pour it down the drain, but do not pour it onto houseplants.

FULL MOON
CRYSTAL QUARTZ
BATTERY CHARGE

It's great to line up your spellwork with the phases of the moon, working for increase during the waxing moon and release during the waning moon, but life doesn't always coincide so easily with this pattern.

What if you need a quick prosperity boost, for example, when the moon is waning? You can plan ahead, by charging a quartz crystal with the power of the Full Moon, which you can then use in a spell at any time.

Quartz crystals act as a "battery" of sorts, storing the energy you charge them with and then releasing it as you direct them to, later on. While you can certainly charge any stone under the light of the Full Moon, quartz is ideal as a "multipurpose" stone, lending its energy to whatever magical aim you're working for.

So whether or not you're planning any spellwork for the next Full Moon, do yourself a favor and charge up your quartz, so you'll be able to use it as needed at any time.

YOU WILL NEED

1 or more quartz crystals

**Bell or chime
(optional)**

+ Of course you'll first need to clean your crystal(s). There are several methods to choose from. Most sources on crystals recommend keeping them under cool running water for 10 minutes for a thorough cleaning. However, some Witches wince at the use of so much water, particularly those living in areas of drought. If you're going to use the crystal for healing purposes, such as in a bath or an elixir, it may be best to go the whole 10 minutes. Otherwise, you can find more environmentally friendly ways of clearing old energy from your stones—such as burying them in sea salt or soil, and rinsing briefly afterward.

+ Direct moonlight and sunlight are both considered to be cleansing as well as charging, so depending on the current energetic state of your crystal(s), you may not feel that a separate cleansing step is necessary.

+ If you want to be thorough, however, try this method: rinse your crystals briefly under water, then clear them with a bell or chime. Hold them under the bell or chime in one hand and ring it with the other. (If you have a wind chime or a Tibetan bell hanging on a porch or doorway, it will work great for this purpose.)

+ Then, lay them out to charge under the light of the Full Moon— either outside, or in a windowsill. (It's fine if they're still wet from the rinsing—let them air dry as they charge!)

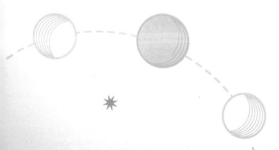

✦ If you like, say the following (or similar) words as you lay out the crystal(s):

"I charge this crystal by
Full Moon's light
For any purpose I shall need.

The energy grows both
strong and bright
My future spellwork will succeed."

✦ The following morning, place the crystal(s) in a special location where you will see them often. If you don't use them within a few weeks, you may want to repeat this charging at the next Full Moon.

FOUR DIRECTIONS BLESSINGS SPELL FOR NEW YEAR

This powerful ritual can be used to kick off manifestations in several areas of your life as you draw on the influences of the four cardinal directions. Each direction is associated with one of the four elements, and therefore the specific magical properties of that element.

The spell can be worked at the conventional New Year—i.e., at the start of the calendar year, or whenever you consider your personal New Year to begin, whether that's the Pagan holiday of Samhain, the festival of Yule, the Chinese New Year, or even your birthday. Whichever date you choose, be sure to first spend some time contemplating what you'd like to bring into your life for the coming year. (If you don't yet have clear goals in mind, try free-writing for awhile to get your ideas flowing.)

Using the table on the opposite page, identify one goal to correspond with each direction, keeping in mind that more than one direction could be applicable. This means you can choose four different goals, or focus the spell on one goal with four different facets.

For example, if you're looking to improve your career options, you might choose North to address the financial aspect, but East can also be invoked for the energy of new beginnings, South for the courage and stamina to carry out your plans, and/or West for washing away any hidden resistance to change.

Once you've settled on your request for each direction, you may want to write them down so they'll be easier to remember during the ritual. (You can also save the paper and refer back to it to check your progress at various points throughout the year.)

FOUR DIRECTIONS/ELEMENTS

TABLE OF CORRESPONDENCE

DIRECTION	ASSOCIATED ELEMENT	AREAS OF MANIFESTATION
NORTH	EARTH	Financial abundance, home and hearth, physical possessions, practical matters
EAST	AIR	Creativity, change, new beginnings, inspiration, clarity of perspective
SOUTH	FIRE	Love, vitality, passion, initiative, courage to follow through on ideas
WEST	WATER	Healing, cleansing, intuition, emotional concerns, psychic and spiritual awareness

**1 white pillar candle
(or a color that has strong
significance for you)**

**Paper and pen/pencil for
writing your goals for the year
(optional)**

≡ INSTRUCTIONS ≡

✦ Start facing North with your feet a few inches apart, back
straight, head held high, elbows at your sides, and palms
facing upward to represent your readiness to receive new
blessings.

✦ Say:

*"With the aid of the Spirits of the North,
this new year brings (goal) into my life."*

✦ Then turn to the East and say:

*"With the aid of the Spirits of the East,
this new year brings (goal) into my life."*

✦ Turn to the South and say:

*"With the aid of the Spirits of the South,
this new year brings (goal) into my life."*

✦ Finally, turn to the West and say:

*"With the aid of the Spirits of the West,
this new year brings (goal) into my life."*

- ✦ Now, light the candle.*

- ✦ Gently pick it up and hold it in both hands as you face North a second time. Summon all the positivity you will feel when your stated goal for North has manifested.

- ✦ Hold this feeling steady while taking three deep breaths (making sure not to blow the candle out when exhaling).

- ✦ Then turn again to the East, South, and West, repeating the process for each direction.

- ✦ Finally, place the candle back on your altar and make one more round of facing each direction, this time standing with your arms raised over your head, palms placed flat together and fingers pointed upward.

- ✦ As you face each direction, say these closing words:

"For this year will be the
most magical I have lived.
Blessed Be."

————

*The pillar candle can be reused after this spell,
for as long as you like until it's spent. However, it's
a good idea to say a few words of gratitude
each time you light and extinguish it.
By the time you've burned the entire candle,
at least a few of the blessings
you've called in will have begun
to manifest!

ELEMENTAL
CHAI CREATIVITY SPELL

This delicious spell results in a magical tea blend that you can enjoy anytime you're seeking creative inspiration. You will call upon the primal co-creative energies of the Elements as you add each spice to the recipe, infusing the blend with their (and your) magical power.

Drink this chai as a ritual when beginning any creative work, letting it enchant you into a flow of new ideas. To add extra magical "oomph," make a colorful label for the jar you'll store the chai in and decorate the lid.

You'll need a loose-leaf tea infuser or empty tea bags to brew this tea. Use a teaspoon to a tablespoon per serving, depending on your preference, and feel free to adjust the amounts listed here.

≡ YOU WILL NEED ≡

- 1 cup loose leaf Assam black tea
- 4 teaspoons anise seed (AIR)
- 2 teaspoons cardamom seeds (WATER)
- 2 tablespoons cinnamon chips (or coarsely grated cinnamon stick) (FIRE)
- 1 tablespoon dried minced ginger (EARTH)

Mortar and pestle

Bowl

Small jar with screw-top lid

Optional Additions:

- 1 tablespoon whole cloves
- 1 teaspoon allspice berries
- 1 teaspoon black peppercorns

+ Place the black tea in the bowl and set aside.

+ Add the anise seed to the mortar. As you do so, say the following (or similar) words:

> *"With the spirit of Air,*
> *I welcome ideas into my creative life."*

+ With the pestle, gently stir in the cardamom seeds, saying:

> *"With the spirit of Water, I tap into the*
> *flow of my creative intuition."*

+ Follow with the cinnamon chips, saying:

> *"With the spirit of Fire,*
> *I spark my passion to create."*

+ Add the ginger, saying:

> *"With the spirit of Earth, I bring new*
> *creation into the physical world."*

+ If there are any other spices you wish to include, add them now.

+ Gently stir the spice mixture into the black tea. Hold the bowl up with both hands and say the following (or similar) words:

> *"With the energy of Spirit that infuses all*
> *things, this tea is charged. Blessed Be."*

+ Transfer the tea blend to the jar, close the lid, and give it a good shake. Enjoy!

CONCLUSION

HOPEFULLY, ON YOUR FIRST BROWSING THROUGH THIS BOOK, you've already found a few spells that grab your interest and suit your purpose. As time goes on, you're likely to find plenty more!

But what if there are several you'd like to try and you can't decide where to start? This is a common—and quite delightful—dilemma! Just don't let the options overwhelm you to the point where you're hesitant to work any magic at all.

In the event that you are struggling to choose a spell to start with, here are a few suggestions:

Let timing be your guide. What phase is the Moon in, currently? Consult a moon calendar if you're unsure, and then use this information to narrow down your choices. Working for increase is generally best during the Moon's waxing days, while spells aimed at banishing or eliminating something unwanted are most effective during the waning Moon.

Reflect on your "wish list," whether that means writing one or simply thinking about the positive changes you'd like to see in your life. Then, choose a goal that you feel not only a strong desire about, but also a fair amount of confidence in your ability to focus your intentions effectively enough for the spellwork to succeed. In other words, don't start with the most challenging aspect of your life unless you know deep down that you now have the power to change it.

Finally, use a bit of magic in your decision-making process. Choose five or more spells that you'd like to try and write their titles down on separate squares of paper. Fold the squares, mix them up in a bowl, and ask the Universe to help you choose the best one to start with. Then close your eyes and trust that your fingers will select the perfect spell!

No matter what your process for selecting spellwork, be sure to enjoy yourself and put your own unique energy into selecting and charging your ingredients, performing the actions, and visualizing the results of your magical efforts. Make a note of any substitutions or other alterations you make to the spells as they are written here, and keep track of the results as they manifest in your life.

Good luck to you, and Blessed Be!

ACKNOWLEDGMENTS

MY DEEPEST THANKS TO MY BIRTH FAMILY AND MY CHOSEN family for their eternal love and support. To Kelli Hutchison for still being a magical presence after all these years. And to the pine tree that dropped a cone on my head that day as I sat pondering the possibilities of writing books about Witchcraft.

As always, it's such a pleasure to work with editor Barbara Berger and rest of the team at Sterling. Thanks to art director Elizabeth Lindy for the beautiful cover design; interior art directors Kevin Ullrich and Christine Heun; Sharon Jacobs for the stunning interior design conception, direction, and layout; production editor Michael Cea; and production manager Krista-Lise Endahl.

PICTURE CREDITS

INDEX

ABOUT THE AUTHOR

LISA CHAMBERLAIN is the successful author of more than twenty books on Wicca and magic, including *Wicca for Beginners*, *Wicca Herbal Magic*, and *Wiccan Kitchen*. Her Wiccan experience has evolved over years from a traditional practice to more eclectic explorations. Her focus is on positive magic that promotes self-empowerment for the good of the whole.

You can find out more at:
wiccaliving.com